When God Gives a Time Out

Joseph R. Greene

PublishAmerica
Baltimore

First printing

All scripture taken from the NEW AMERICAN STANDARD BIBLE, Copyright 1960, 1962, 1968, 1971, 1973, 1975, 1977, 1995 by The Lockman Foundation. Used by Permission.

ISBN: 1-4241-0395-9
PUBLISHED BY PUBLISHAMERICA, LLLP
www.publishamerica.com
Baltimore

Printed in the United States of America

This book is dedicated to God, Wendi, Patrick, Abigail and Isaiah.

Table of Contents

Part 5 - When God No Longer Needs to Give a "Time Out"

Part 1
"Go Sit on the Stairs"
The What and How of "Time Outs"

An Introduction to "Time Outs"

If you are a parent, you have probably experienced what I recently witnessed. At a local store, a young boy was bursting with energy. Every inch of his body was in motion. All this chaotic movement didn't seem to have a purpose other than expending energy. He jumped on one foot, then the other. Soon he began to shake his head from side to side as if saying, "No." Perhaps he wanted the outside world to mirror his topsy-turvy condition on the inside. The child then climbed on the front of the carriage for a ride. The mother's call to calm down fell on senses more focused on doing than listening. Since the ride wasn't fast enough, the child hopped off the carriage so that he could touch everything. He grabbed at everything in range of his small hands, trying to do what the big people do when they shop. The exasperated mother pulled the child into the center of the aisle to put the distractions out of reach and told him, "Stop touching things without asking first!" But this child had to DO something, there were so many stimuli in this place and they all called out to be engaged. As the scene reached its climax, the boy cried out, "Look, a plate just like the one we have at home!" He snatched up a plate to see if it was indeed the same. Halfway through the motion, the child remembered that he wasn't supposed to touch without asking and his attention-divided fingers let go of the plate. The frustrated mother had reached her limit. Mustering all her patience, the mother sternly told the boy to go sit on the bench for a "time out." The mother cleaned up the broken shards and said something like, "You have to listen to me. You can get hurt and you hurt other people's things when you can't calm down and listen to me."

Is this scene a familiar one for you? Perhaps, like me, you empathized and felt an immediate kinship with this frazzled mother. This scenario is all too familiar for me, since I am usually that frazzled parent and the active child is usually my youngest boy, Isaiah. Yes, Isaiah is very familiar with "time outs." I don't give him "time outs" because I want him to be a little robot, nor do I want to be a drill sergeant. I am proud of the fact that Isaiah wants to engage the world around him and do everything with gusto. But for his own well being, especially when he is little, he needs to be able to hear my voice and respond to it, even when he is in the midst of engaging a world of stimuli. As an adult, I can see consequences of actions better (hopefully). I can see the "big picture" and keep things in perspective more than a child (usually). Through my relationship with my son, I build these qualities in him: One trip to the store at a time, one "time out" after another. At first, this process looks like Isaiah simply doing what he is told, but eventually it becomes more internal. After five years of "time outs" Isaiah sometimes asks if he can do something before he acts in order to discern if the choice is a wise one. One day, he will be able to see the bigger picture for himself and from different perspectives. He will desire things that are truly valuable and have healthy priorities. This process of handing down mature qualities can't take place if he is too distracted to hear my voice. So Isaiah needs a "time out" to refocus his attention on my voice and remove the distractions. In this process the relationship between father and son takes center stage and the growth process can continue.

Whenever I see a child in "time out" I am reminded of my children's behavior as well as my own. "Apples don't fall far from the tree" goes the saying, and like Isaiah, I am very familiar with "time outs." There is a certain rush to engaging the world around me, manipulating things I come in contact with, doing big and important things like my Heavenly Father. But without the nurturing connection to the Father, the loving watch care of the Father, I can get hurt and hurt others. The qualities that will make me a well-balanced man of character are handed down and best cultivated through my relationship with my Heavenly Father, not by just doing the things that make me look more like "a big person." God is all too familiar with this behavior in both me and you—this is why God gives "time outs." He gives "time outs" to remove the distractions so that we can hear His voice again.

In America we increasingly live in a culture that needs a "time out." Many children grow up in a family where a parent is physically missing. Many more grow up in a family where the parents are emotionally missing. Many children don't know how to hear a parent's voice, and if they do, they don't trust it. Instead of seeking a parental voice, our culture seeks more and more stimuli. A booming movie, video game, and sports industry testify to the fact that we desire to be distracted, entertained, and get a vicarious rush. The most important thing is what you do and that you are always doing *something*. We are a culture of children bouncing about in the aisles of America; chocolate smeared on our faces, breaking a plate here, running into other shoppers' carriages there. We don't know why, but we just feel the need to move and when we come off our sugar high, we collapse, sobbing at the chaos. We thought we did a lot, but looking around we only see broken stuff and the things we were focused on seemed to have vanished like a vapor. But when we leave the store empty-handed and put our exhausted, frustrated heads on the pillow, one thing remains. The Father.

Is this what it takes for us to finally stop doing stuff and listen to the Father? A frustrated burnout that leaves us empty on the inside? For some, this is what it takes. But, for others, God thankfully (although we may not feel thankful at the time) gives "time outs."

Questions to Ponder

How are you like the hyper child in the store?

Do you always feel the need to be doing something? What kinds of task do you spend most of your time on?

Time Out!
What Do You Mean "Time Out?"

I use the term "time out" because God does in concept what we see so many parents literally doing to their children. It all boils down to the fact that the child is not listening. They may be doing something they are not supposed to, or just doing something other than listening. The parent makes the child cease all activity. The child must now sit on the stairs, or in a special chair, with nothing to do except listen.

I will speak about the specific "time outs" God has given me in subsequent chapters. In general though, a "time out" is when God so controls the situation that you have no choice but to stop doing a certain thing, or stop doing everything. Something is getting in the way of hearing God's voice and He is making you sit quietly until you are ready to listen. Are you in a relationship and suddenly circumstances cause you to cease contact with that person? Perhaps it is a "time out." Have you ever had a job that kept you real busy and you either can't do that job for a time or get permanently laid off? Perhaps a "time out." Can you remember any period in your life when you were stuck or just unable to do a certain thing? Again, God may have been giving you a "time out." This feeling of being stuck reminds me of how my wife would give a "time out" to our kids when they were toddlers. On occasion, Wendi would tell one of our children to go sit on the stair, but they wouldn't go. She would then take that child to the stair and hold them very firmly. Of course they would struggle to break free, but they were stuck. Eventually, they calmed down and were ready to listen. God will hold us on the stair until we stop squirming. We want to quickly get out of the "time out," but God must talk to us about the situation so that we are better able to deal with it the next time. God can bring you to a place were you are stuck financially. Is He holding you in a "time out" so that you will listen to Him concerning how you manage your money? God can bring single people to a place were they just can't seem to get a date. He may be trying to get that single person to listen to what He has to say about relationships. Whether it is a specific area of your life, as in these examples, or your entire life, God gives "time outs" so that he can lovingly parent you to a place of maturity.

Not every instance of being stuck is a "time out" from God. Every time such an occasion comes up, however, we can be proactive and consider it a "time out" and listen for the voice of God.

The history of Israel was full of "time outs." The book of Judges records the cycle of God giving Israel "time outs" by allowing invaders to oppress Israel. As Israel was stuck and unable to do the things they once enjoyed, they cried out to God and listened to His voice. When they listened to the Lord, God ended the "time out" by sending a deliverer. Before long, Israel again stopped listening to God and "everyone did what was right in his own eyes." (Judges 21: 25) During this time there was much religious activity and much was getting done, but all the activity was not a result of hearing God's voice. People were doing what seemed right to them and that is when they got into trouble.

When we do whatever seems right, we also get into trouble. We listen to the voice in our head or the voices in our culture and do whatever seems right. We don't listen to God, because we assume that we already have the direction we need. Israel was directed towards idolatry and false religion. These practices distracted them from hearing their Heavenly Father's voice and hurt their relationship with Him. Christians are directed towards the idols of success, or popularity, or esteem. Like the Israelite's idolatry, these practices distract us from hearing God's voice and hurt our relationship with Him. If necessary, our Father in Heaven will bring us through a cycle of "time outs" until we realize that our relationship with Him must be the driving force behind all that we do in life.

"Time outs" seem punitive, but they are ultimately aimed at producing maturity and growth in God's people. The Babylonian captivity is the central "time out" in the history of Israel. Even after the period of judges, Israel continued to listen to the voice of idolatrous priests, false prophets and corrupt kings. Israel waged wars, followed laws, and did "religion" like all the other nations—and that was the problem. Like the other nations they didn't function out of a relationship with

God or from hearing His voice. The Israelites were God's children and enjoyed a special relationship to God. Instead of living in that special relationship, they chose to live like other nations. God gave Israel a seventy-year "time out" in Babylon and when they returned, pagan idolatry never again distracted them from hearing God's voice. Many other distractions and subtle idolatries of the mind would arise, but Israel put away pagan idolatry and the desire to do things like other nations. The "punishment" of the captivity was a national "time out" that was aimed at returning Israel to a close relationship with God. In captivity, the Israelites could no longer do civil, social, or religious things like they were accustomed to. Instead, they were stuck in Babylon. Did they enjoy being away from home and in captivity? Absolutely not. "Time outs" may not be enjoyable, but they are a way for our Heavenly Father to hone our relationship with Him and mature us. God's motive for a "time out" is not revenge. "Time outs" are a way for God to bring about the intimacy and growth He has planned for His children. Concerning Israel's "time out" in Babylon, the Prophet Jeremiah says,

> "For thus says the LORD, 'When seventy years have been completed for Babylon, I will visit you and fulfill My good word to you, to bring you back to this place. For I know the plans that I have for you,' declares the LORD, 'plans for welfare and not for calamity to give you a future and a hope. Then you will call upon Me and come and pray to Me, and I will listen to you. You will seek Me and find Me when you search for Me with all your heart. I will be found by you,' declares the LORD, 'and I

will restore your fortunes and will gather you from all the nations and from all the places where I have driven you,' declares the LORD, 'and I will bring you back to the place from where I sent you into exile.'" (Jeremiah 29: 10-14)

God's plan, although it seemed cruel, effected the necessary change in the Israelites. After (and during) the Babylonian "time out" Israel called upon God. The relationship of Israel listening to God and God listening to Israel was restored for a time. No longer did Israel seek to do things like the other nations. Instead they sought God. They sought the Father's voice instead of the competing voices that surrounded them. Although "time outs" aren't fun, know that God's ultimate plan for you is for good. He wants to be in relationship with His children and sometimes we need a "time out" so we can hear that loving plan.

Questions to Ponder

As you read this chapter did any occasion in your life immediately come to mind as a possible "time out"?

Can you think of any other "time outs" recorded in the Bible?

Assumptions

You have probably already recognized that I hold assumptions that most people in our Western culture don't hold. I am assuming that God wants an active relationship with His creation. Sure, most people believe in God, but a God who is absent. Like the Deists of early America, our culture thinks of God as a watchmaker who made and wound the whole universe like a watch and will not return until time has wound down.

Outside of the Christian subculture, God is not thought of as a player in solving problems, planning the day, or even giving guidance in relationships or finances. God is considered to be like an old grandfather living out of state. We like him because we are related to him and he seems nice. But to be honest, he is rather harmless and we don't know him that well. What we know of him is mostly from stories that other people tell us about him.

Not surprisingly, the Bible, Jesus, and Christianity have assumptions about God that differ greatly from our culture. The entire Bible assumes that God wants to be known by His creation. The whole idea of a "Bible" is that God wanted to reveal something about Himself and inspired the biblical writers to write. As we read the Bible it becomes clear that the God portrayed in the scriptures is a God who wants a relationship with His people.

Why did God create people in the first place? Because He was bored? Because He needed some maids or butlers? No, because the love and relationship that exists within the Trinity is so abundant that God wanted it to spill out into other beings. He made us to love us and the reason God reveals Himself in scripture is so we can know Him. God further revealed Himself in Jesus so that we could know Him in an even more personal way. The New Testament describes how Jesus died for humanity because our sins separated us from God. Our sins prevent us from being in proper relationship with God and Jesus wiped out our sins for eternity so that we could be in a right relationship with God. In several places in the scriptures we are said to have been "reconciled to God" through Jesus. The only context I know of someone using the term "reconcile" is when they are speaking of relationship, like when a husband and wife or a parent and child are reconciled. The Bible clearly assumes that we were made to hear, enjoy, and love our Almighty Creator.

Jesus summed up God's plan for humanity in John 17:3. He said, "This is eternal life, that they may know You, the only true God, and Jesus Christ whom You have sent." Eternity is about knowing Jesus and knowing God. Jesus succinctly stated that we were given eternal souls in order to have a relationship with the God who is in relationship within Himself, within the Trinity. Friends, eternal life doesn't start when we die. Do you have an eternal soul now? Then you have eternal life now. The question is whether you have eternal life with God or apart from God.

In another part of the Bible, Jesus gives us the whole of scripture in a nutshell. In Matthew 22:37-40 Jesus said,

"'You shall love the Lord your God with all your heart, and with all your soul, and with all your mind.' This is the great and foremost commandment. The second is like it, 'You shall love your neighbor as yourself.' On these two commandments depend the whole Law and the Prophets."

Why did Jesus say that all the commandments, the miraculous stories, and prophetic directives of scripture depend on loving God? Our default way of living, the living assumption of all humanity, is to pursue what we love. We can *know* the Bible inside and out, but to *live* the Bible we need love. As the twelfth century monk, Bernard of Clairvaux, said, "True love…has its reward in what it loves. For if you seem to love something, but love it for the sake of something else, you actually love what you are pursuing as your real end, not that which is a means to it."[1] The "why" behind our actions can usually be traced to love. Our lives do not match the Bible when we use God or people to acquire another love. If, however, we are in a loving relationship with God and with people, all the commandments will take care of themselves naturally. Idolatry, murder, stealing, lying, adultery are symptoms of a heart that does not love God and people as much as something else. This law of love is why God seeks to cultivate love and relationships in our lives. The law of pursuing what we love is the reason that God give us a "time out." The law of love is the reason we cannot, and God does not, settle for religious activity.

Unfortunately many Christians don't live a life that assumes that God is most interested in a loving relationship. Too many Christians give the impression that God wants us to do a certain set of religious activities. Not only do many Christians carry this assumption, many Christians are more comfortable with a religious check-list than with a relationship. We want a list of things to do and goals to meet. We can deal with facts to analyze, but this whole relationship thing is too process-oriented! Relationships are not something we can put in a box and have all figured out by performing a certain set of tasks by rote. Nor is love a duty; love is a heartfelt commitment towards intimacy and better relationship. Relationships grow and change and involve a give and take between two parties. We can not fake love and relationships for too long. Duties, knowledge; those things we can get done. But love and relationships never end, they only grow or shrink. This is eternal life, that we know God and know Jesus. The Bible assumes that God wants a relationship with us and Jesus assumes that God wants a relationship with us. It is time for *Christians* to assume that God wants a relationship with us. In this active relationship God is the wise one, the powerful one. As God proved by sending Jesus, God can and will do whatever necessary to remove the barriers that interfere with our hearing of Him. One of the ways that God sharpens our hearing and sharpens our relationship with Him is by giving us a "time out."

Joseph R. Greene

Questions to Ponder

What are your assumptions about God and God's relationship to the creation?

How do your assumptions about Jesus and the Bible color your view of God?

How do these assumptions affect:
    your overall concept of God?
    your religious practice?
    the way you live?

Ecclesiastes 5:1 states, "Guard your steps as you go to the house of God and draw near *to listen* rather than to offer the sacrifice of fools; for they do not know they are doing evil." How do your assumptions about a relationship with God fit into this warning?

Be Careful Where You Are Headed —You May Actually Get There.

I am a doer. When I first met my wife, Wendi, I was in college at the University of Maryland in the Washington, D.C. area and I had a seven-year plan. This plan spelled out what I was going to achieve over the next several years. I planned to complete my undergraduate degree with a 4.0 GPA, while interning in the nation's capitol. I was in a Military Intelligence Army reserve unit next to the National Security Agency (NSA) and was looking into some part-time work for the NSA. This scenario would have set me up nicely to be accepted into an ivy-league law school to specialize in international law. After law school the seven years would be completed and after taking stock, I could make a new plan. To me, relationships were secondary to accomplishing goals. I let Wendi know that my plan was in place and that where our relationship was going (to marriage or elsewhere) depended on the status of my plan.

I followed my plan for about a year and a half with quite a bit of success. My plan changed, however, when

God brought me to my first "time out." God gave me a sneak peak into what would happen if I actually achieved everything in my plan. I asked myself, "If my wildest dreams came true, if I become a high level advisor on the national level, or if I am elected to the legislature, then so what?" Even if I achieved all those goals, they would be gone—forgotten within a generation. If I achieved my wildest dreams, I would have achieved nothingness. This revelation didn't come about subtly. It was driven home by a Bible cult that I had started hanging around with. (I describe this association more in subsequent chapters.) God knew that I needed a LOUD wake up call.

After a short time of looking at things through an eternal perspective I knew that God was the only thing of any permanence and the only thing worth devoting my life to. I soon realized that I wanted to devote my life to God, but not this cult. In the cult's eyes you couldn't do one without the other. Rather confused and feeling that I didn't want to follow my plan or this cult anymore, I left. I went back home to live with my parents. For the next couple of months I was in "time out." God took away everything I was doing. I no longer had a plan except to abandon my old plan because it was worthless. I didn't have a clear grasp of what the Bible really said or what God wanted me to do next. Away from college and all I had lived for, I spent the subsequent few months pouring over the Bible for myself. I really focused on the voice of the Father and my relationship with Him grew. This was my first "time out" and it felt like the hardest time of my life while I was going through it. But in hindsight, I am so thankful for that "time out." I was so focused on doing, on achieving, on following the American dream that I was actually throwing my life and relationship with the Father away. God was trying to tell me this truth for some time, but I couldn't hear him. I was too busy doing stuff. I needed a "time out" and that is exactly what I got.

I am struck by how deaf we (I) can be to God's voice. Often it is only after we are in a "time out" that we re-hear what God was saying to us. Much like a parent-to-child conversation, our brains pick up the words on a semi-conscious level, but the connection doesn't go any deeper than the physical senses. When a child is alone and quiet (perhaps a "time out") she can then remember and re-hear what she couldn't hear because of the distraction of activity. When God pulled back the curtain of my future, showing me the futility of my grand plan, He spoke to me through King Solomon, the writer of the Biblical book, Ecclesiastes. I would have to say that Ecclesiastes made the greatest impact on me when I was beginning my "time out." In Ecclesiastes, Solomon wrote about obtaining all the greatest things that the world had to offer. He found that they were all meaningless without God. What's amazing is God had been telling me that my own plan was meaningless long before He even put me in "time out." I was just too distracted to hear Him. The truth of my deafness came to light some months after I withdrew from school when I found a poem inspired by Ecclesiastes. Although I don't remember it specifically, I assume I read Ecclesiastes when I first entered college. Shortly after, I wrote this poem for a poetry class. This poem was written months before I was put into "time out" and really listened to God's voice. This is the poem:

To Solomon the wisest greatest king,
who lengthy searched and found no world repose.
I give you thanks, and songs of yours I sing,
with hopes to see the truth your tale still shows.
Uncountable, desolate, expansive treasures,
Attainments, worldly, grasped in flesh fingers,
Your harems spilling sensory pleasures,
The wisdom stirred your soul, empty lingers,
Does power held in hand fulfill purpose?
when flesh is torn off, leaving bone and nerves?
How long to dwell on a rocky surface,
where time proceeds, to see Mammon be served.
Time's finale will come, it draws too nigh,
Were birds constructing nests, or did they fly?

This poem shows two things. First, I am not a poet. Second, I was too busy doing big and important things to hear the Father's message. I was later able to hear the exact same message when I was in my "time out." Knowing the history, it is comical to read this poem. I had read God's message in Ecclesiastes and had even written a poem about it. I really did not hear, or receive, the message, however. Ecclesiastes inspired me to write this poem, but I was deaf to God's voice. In the fourth line, I wrote, "With hopes to see the truth your tale still shows." On one level, I had heard and seen the message of Ecclesiastes—but past the physical senses I was blind and deaf to the truth that God was speaking to me through this scripture. In hindsight, it was clear that the Father was trying to speak directly and firmly to me. I was too busy doing stuff, trying to achieve the plan and manipulate the world around me. God gave me a "time out" a year after I wrote this poem because if I continued to ignore His message in Ecclesiastes I would have gone down a path that I would have regretted till my death.

The message of Ecclesiastes is one of the first truths all of us doers need to *really* hear. King Solomon tells how he achieved wealth, wisdom, women and power. His assessment of it all:

> "Then I became great and increased more than all who preceded me in Jerusalem. My wisdom also stood by me. All that my eyes desired I did not refuse them. I did not withhold my heart from any pleasure, for my heart was pleased because of all my labor and this was my reward for all my labor. Thus I considered all my activities which my hands had done and the labor which I had exerted, and behold all was vanity and striving after wind and there was no profit under the sun."

(Ecclesiastes 2: 9-11)

God can see the big picture and He sees where all of our doing will lead us. Solomon's deeds led him to be the greatest king of Israel in terms of physical things. God showed him that all of it was meaningless. He called it vanity and striving after the wind. What a picture this metaphor paints! You can exert tremendous energy chasing after the wind in order to catch it. Although it is impossible to catch the wind, even if you succeeded all you would have is a handful of air, which is what you had already. All that sweat, the frantic running, the falling and getting back up, the gritty determination, the training to get fast enough, all of it and you don't have anything more than when you started! A handful of wind. A handful of nothing.

Perhaps you are like Solomon and feel like you are going down a path of meaninglessness. God can show you where your path leads. God longs for us to listen so that He can guide us to a permanent, valuable, and meaningful place. But will we listen? *Can* we listen? I couldn't listen. I not only read God's message to me in the book of Ecclesiastes, but I even wrote a poem about it. Despite all this, I still couldn't listen to what God was trying to tell me.

Do you have a "time out" in your life to ask yourself (or better still, to ask God) where all your doing will lead you? Be careful where you're going—you may actually get there. King of Israel, a political big wig, financial stability, they are all places that disappear like the wind when the night time of life comes. *Taking* a "time out" to hear the eternal call is always easier than being given a "time out." Either way, go to the Father of wisdom and He will lead you onto the permanent path of meaning.

Questions to Ponder

As you look at the direction of your life, where are you headed?

When you are at the end of life what do you hope to have achieved? Will any of these achievements last?

If God wanted to tell you something right now would you be able to hear Him?

What distracts you the most from hearing God?

Part 2
The Compulsion to Do

We Are In Deep Do-Do

Why do we do what we do? There are some conscious and some not so conscious reasons for our choices. Parts 2 and 3 look at many of the forces behind what we do. No matter the elements involved in our choice of *what* to do, the goal of a Christian life is to do *everything* from God's guidance. Choosing what to do out of a relationship with God may sound difficult and a bit restrictive, but the Bible promises great rewards for following God in our actions. We are promised intimacy with God, deeper meaning to life, power, and inner peace.

God actually wants what is best for us and He desires to bless us by fulfilling His promises to His followers. We can't follow God's voice into these blessings if we aren't listening. This deafness is why God gives "time outs." We are busy and the activity is distracting us because our choices are coming from a source other than God. We are choosing to do many things for many reasons, but none of this activity is from the Father's instruction. God gives us a "time out" so that we can hear His voice once again and our actions can spring from an interaction with God.

Wouldn't it be great if all the things we did actually drew us closer to God instead of distracting us from Him? God wants you and me to experience this blessing.

Part 2 will look at the many reasons why we do what we do, why we end up getting into deep "do-do", and why so many are hearing impaired and need a "time out."

Giving You Your Do

We live in a culture of doers. Where I live in the Northeast when asked, "How are you doing?" a common response is, "Keeping busy." The assumption is that this person is well because to be busy is what life is about. Most people turn on the radio the moment they get in the car, or turn on the television as soon as they get home. There must be stimuli, something to busy the airwaves around them. Being entertained is one way of keeping busy. When we listen to the radio, watch television, see a movie, play video games, watch sports, we are being entertained, also known as "keeping busy." The entertainment industry is huge because our need to be busy with stimuli is huge. In our culture, being entertained qualifies as doing something positive. If someone is asked what they did on Sunday afternoon and the response is, "Watched the football game," that person will get no strange or quizzical looks from anybody. If that same person answers, "I sat by the river and watched the water," that person will get a few raised eyebrows and the title "Weirdo." Is a watcher of pigskin doing any more than a watcher of water? We live in a culture of doers but we aren't driven to do everything, just those things that society holds in highest regard. Whatever we choose to do, if it is held in regard, we let people know. There are bumper stickers, T-shirts, throw rugs, and hats proclaiming that we go fishing or play golf more than we talk to our wives. In a culture of doers what you do is almost (but not quite) as important as how busy you are.

The importance we place on what we do is even more magnified when considering our occupation. Who hasn't met new people and within five minutes someone asks, "What do you do?" It is one of the first questions new acquaintances ask one another because of the importance our culture places on what we do, especially for a "living." In other cultures, your family background is inquired about first. Have you ever been asked, "So, what's your lineage?" I haven't, but I know I have been asked countless times, "What do you do?"

When you are in a "time out" you aren't doing much of anything according to this world's values. You may not even know where you are going next. You have no answer to the question, "What do you do?" You can't even say, "Well, I am preparing to switch gears and go into..." I remember in my first "time out," when I dropped out of college for a while, old friends would ask, "So what are you doing?" I would say, "I'm just reading my Bible, trying to discern what God would have me do next." What they would hear, "I am doing nothing." In our culture, reading the Bible and tuning into God's voice doesn't qualify as doing something. Even in many Christian subcultures it doesn't qualify as a positive endeavor. Nevertheless, when we are in a "time out" and we are trying to tune into the voice of God, we are engaged in an activity that is life transforming and eternally meaningful.

In another "time out" I was kept from doing formal ministry or holding any secular employment and when people asked me what I did, I would say, "I watch my kids during the day." What people actually heard, "I am doing nothing." Although this has changed a lot over recent years, raising kids as your sole occupation doesn't actually count as doing something—especially if you are male. Sometimes I told people about my last ministry because I didn't want to be judged as not doing anything by our culture's standards. Deep in my heart I had not accepted the fact that my relationship with God and following His will were my most important tasks. During that particular "time out," God wanted me to take care of my children and take care of my relationship with Him. I needed to learn that no matter what stimuli this world dubs as valuable, no matter what tasks vie for my attention, the most important task before me is to listen to my Father's voice. If I can't listen on my own, for my well being, He will give me a "time out" to cultivate the relationship.

Why do we choose to do what we do? Do our choices spring from our relationship with God and His values—or from the values of our culture? Why do we believe the hype that we must always be busy doing certain activities? As Christians, we say that our beliefs come from the Bible, but what we choose to do on a daily basis seems to come more from our culture. What we do minute by minute and our goals for the day, these are given to us. We are given our "do" by the voice of society.

Joseph R. Greene

Will we accept the hype? If enough people start doing or endorsing something then our minds tell us that the thing has to be of some value and we want to do it so that we will be valued too. The problem is that very few things live up to their billing. We go through life thinking we need to have a certain occupation or to be entertained a certain way. When we finally have what we seek, and it doesn't satisfy, we move on to another set of promises. We get in a rat race of believing the hype and when that thing doesn't satisfy we try something else, whatever society is currently endorsing. Worse yet, we settle for the temporary, tiny pleasures instead of seeking the deep, abiding satisfaction that only God can provide.

My first experience with believing the hype was when I was about nine years old. I was looking through a comic book when there they were—Sea monkeys.[2] The picture was actually a drawing of a father, mother, and two kid sea monkeys. They were pink with webbed hands and feet and they looked much like people but with knobby antennae on their heads instead of hair. I imagined having a fish tank in my room with this charming little sea monkey family living in it. Every day I could check on their well-being. I imagined that these little sea monkeys, while not as intelligent as people, would communicate in their own charming way.

I eagerly sent away for the sea monkeys using my saved up allowance. I checked the mail every day as I waited for my sea monkey family to arrive. Finally, after a couple of weeks, they arrived! I poured the little packet of eggs into the water and followed the other directions. In a week or so, the instructions said that my sea monkeys would hatch. Sure enough, in about a week I started seeing some movement. The "monkeys" were so tiny that they looked like little water fleas. I reasoned that they would soon grow and that this strange look was just a stage in their development. Another week went by, and then another, and instead of changing into something that looked more like a monkey, one by one they died— all of them.

My father explained to me that those little creatures were brine shrimp, tiny ocean creatures that look like water fleas. I exclaimed, "But what about the picture in the magazine? The picture showed the little house that they would build to live in! I thought they looked like humans!" My father said, "We tried to tell you. When people are trying to sell you something, it is usually not as good as it seems."

I felt so cheated. What bothered me wasn't the saved up allowance. My disappointment came from putting my hope in hype. The hype didn't deliver any satisfaction and the hype lasted only a week and then died.

My father was wise to the hype and tried to share his wisdom about the sea monkeys. I didn't listen. How could so many satisfied customers, as the advertisement said, be wrong? The hype of doing something valuable by people's standards trumped the value of hearing the wisdom of my father's voice. Our society is trying to gives us our "do." Will we believe the hype and "do the do" or will we tune into the wise voice of our Heavenly Father?

I don't want to be an extreme dualist and contend that our culture is totally corrupt. There are threads of wisdom woven into the fabric of our society. While the overarching theme of our culture is to keep busy, there is a sense that this doesn't always apply in the context of relationships. If you have ever read the personal ads, you come across some statements that would seem strange on a bumper sticker or even on television, but are common in the ads. A common statement in the personal ads is, "I enjoy walks on the beach and long talks." I have never read that on a T-Shirt or bumper sticker—only in the personals. Many people still understand that the key to a relationship is connection and time spent with the loved one. What is done is not important, the connection is.

In Christian speak, we talk about having a "personal relationship" with God or Jesus, but our churches seem to follow a task list. There is one list for the church body to perform together and one list that you should do independently. The lists have tasks such as: buy new pews, organize a revival meeting, set up for the missions council and summer camp, or have good attendance at the weekly pot luck. As Christians, and as the church, we often do things in the same manner and with the same value system as the prevailing culture. Instead of God giving us our "do," the surrounding culture gives us our "to do" list. We are good at organizing and getting things done. Long talks and walks on the beach don't get things done, so we focus on the tasks.

Many people forget how they fell in love with their spouse. Long talks and holding hands on the beach gives way to getting things done, things like: doing over the kitchen, achieving financial stability . . . keeping busy. Our churches, and many people in them, perform many tasks but have forgotten how they fell in love with God. In Revelation, Jesus addresses the church at Ephesus in this way,

"I know your deeds and your toil and perseverance, and that you cannot tolerate evil men, and you put to the test those who call themselves apostles, and they are not, and you found them to be false; and you have perseverance and have endured for My name's sake, and have not grown weary. But I have this against you, that you have left your first love. Therefore remember from where you have fallen, and repent and do the deeds you did at first; or else I am coming to you and will remove your lampstand out of its place—unless you repent." (Revelation 2:2-5)

Just like the church in Ephesus, we are great at "toiling," "not tolerating evil men," and "putting people who call themselves apostles to the test" and not "growing weary." But we leave our first love, and the deeds that made us fall in love—holding hands on the beach and long talks with God. We are much like the Ephesian church indeed. But we have a choice. We can repent and return to the deeds that made us fall in love at first. We can make connection to God (with all the long talks, walks, and "time outs" that connection entails) the most important thing that we do.

One reason that the divorce rate in America is so high is couples who started out with the idealism of love and long talks, end up being swept up in the hype to do. Both spouses are supposed to be doing a career, doing a hobby, and doing entertainment. There is no time for long talks. Intimacy is lost and neither can hear what the other person is really saying anymore. Husband and wife just can't seem to communicate and they talk in different directions. The relationship fails because they left their first love. The love of connection was usurped by the over-hyped love of doing. This estrangement from one's first love also happens to the church and those of us in it. Will we return to loving God and doing those things that foster our relationship with Him? Will we take a "time out" to walk and talk with God?

Questions to Ponder

What tasks are regarded as most important by your upbringing and culture?

In what ways has your culture already affected your choices of what to do in life?

What are some tasks that you consider valuable that your culture does not?

Do you have a "Sea monkey" story? When did you buy into the hype? In what ways do you still believe the hype?

Where do you get your spiritual "to do" list? Where does your church get its spiritual 'to do" list?

How can you better cultivate your relationship with God? What tasks need to be scrapped? What activities would be helpful?

Do the Do

Keeping busy is so entrenched in our culture that everyone is affected to some degree. We all tend to be more focused on tasks than relationships. Performing a task is a concrete goal that is measurable. Usually, we know when the task is complete, when we have met our goal, and when we can move on. Relationships are more process oriented and they really don't end. Because they don't really end, relationships seem less pressing, or urgent, than tasks. Because the task has a deadline, we do the task and put the relationship on hold. Another reason we gravitate towards tasks is that relationships involve at least two parties and all the variables that go along with each one. So what is nice and tidy and wrapped with a little bow today, may be an all out fistfight tomorrow. It is much less messy to concentrate on tasks, so that is how most of us operate. Yes, some of us are more task-oriented than others, but I think most people have had a time in their life (or their whole life) when they felt the need to "do the do." During these times God may intervene and give us a "time out."

There are two kinds of "doers": the "achiever" and the "busybody." The busybody is always busy doing home projects, visiting people, hobbies, exercising, work, and the list goes on and on. The point, however, is simple. The busybody must always keep busy to feel alive. The goal of the doing isn't as important as the doing itself. As long as there is something to do, the busybody can be quite relaxed and content. In fact, when busybodies actually get a handle on life and they aren't busy, they go seeking trouble. I think of one of my busybody friends who bought an old Jeep. If you need a constant source of tasks, buy an old Jeep. The last owner probably beat the heck out of that poor vehicle. As expected the Jeep provided hours of hands on entertainment on blocks in the driveway. When my friend finally got rid of the Jeep, his life started to coast along rather nicely. I guess that was the problem. Shortly after selling his Jeep he moved into a fixer upper house. (The only thing that needs more work than a fixer upper Jeep is a fixer upper house). Busybodies need to be busy with a constant string of tasks to feel alive. Achievers see all this activity without a defined goal as pointless. Achievers can actually appear to be lazy to some busybodies. Achievers have a specific goal in mind, and they are so focused on achieving it, that they may do little else. Achievers need to be striving towards a big goal or task to feel alive.

You have probably seen the difference between a busybody and an achiever mentality at the beach. There are two kids building separate sand castles. One, the busybody, is using a small shell to dig up sand. Then he uses his hand. Rather quickly, he starts collecting little rocks and shells to fortify the wall. Basically whatever is close the child uses and the child goes from building a tower, to building a moat, to just digging a big hole, to making a large sea wall. Building a sand "castle" for this child is really a vague term that means manipulating sand in some way.

The other child, an achiever, starts by using his hand, but quickly stops. He sees that this method is inadequate. His small hand cannot move enough earth. The child quietly sits for a few minutes surveying his plot of land. He is planning. He doesn't even start building his castle for some time. In fact, the busybody child has almost moved onto something else by the time this achiever child even starts. But when he starts, oh boy, does he start. He has secured a real shovel, from the private house across the fence. He has enlisted his father and older sister to help dig a mammoth moat. He has borrowed pre-fab plastic pails already in the shape of ramparts. Other enlisted helpers bring in buckets of shells and long strings of kelp to fortify the walls. As the crew puts the materials in place, the child directs. When things aren't "castle" enough for him, or at least the image he has in his head, he changes them.

Which child are you most like? Do you like to tie up a lot of different little tasks — the busybody? Or do you like to do something big, one large task, that takes a lot of planning — the achiever? While our culture may esteem the achiever type more, both kinds of doers can be equally compulsive, equally distracted from hearing God's voice. Of course, when I speak of types of doers in these derogatory terms I have the sinful state in mind. When activity is an outflow of our close relationship with God, then God can use both the achiever and busybody types for the glory of His kingdom. Those with the achiever mentality can have that quality redeemed and they can use their mindset to develop plans to meet a large kingdom sized task. The busybody can be redeemed so that the many small parts of God's plan (that together make up a grand undertaking) aren't overlooked. They specialize in making sure the trees aren't lost in the forest. God has designed us differently so that the redeemed planners (formerly known as achievers) need the redeemed specializers (formerly known as busybodies) and vice versa.

The interdependence of the achiever and busybody is well documented in the dog eat dog corporate business world of compulsive doing. This interdependence is competitive and people use one another to achieve goals. In the business world the achiever and busybody can reluctantly agree to use one another, but this cooperation usually exists in the context of competition with other companies.

In business, achievers tend to use people to see their plans fulfilled more than busybodies, but busybodies do it too. In both cases, relationships with our fellow man take a backseat to getting things done. Unfortunately, this mindset exists in the church. Starting with a "purpose driven" mindset[3], a well-meaning pastor runs his church ragged trying to achieve church growth. Because the people don't fit what tasks need to be done, they are forced into ministries that don't match their make up. Accountability becomes "what have you done for me and the church growth plan lately" instead of "how have you been cultivating your connection with God and people?" In other cases, a church may seem healthy, but that appearance is due to the achievers and the busybodies realizing that they can get more done by cooperating. People may think such a church is more spiritual when in fact the church is simply savvier in organizational efficiency. The focus is still on doing more and getting bigger. This same cooperation is achieved in the business world apart from the Spirit. The result is a church that gets a lot done—a big, impressive sand castle. But eventually the tide comes in and washes away the big sand castles as well as the little ones. When the tide comes, what remains are the relationships we made while building the castle. Of course, if relationships took a back seat to performing tasks then we are bankrupt indeed. But if the making sprung from a love of the Father and love of people then we still have just as much sand, but now we have relationship. God knows what is permanent and God has a vision for His church. When the church needs a "time out," God can give one. If your church has plateaued or seems stuck, perhaps God is giving the church a "time out" to listen to HIS vision for the church. His vision is for people to be in a love relationship with Jesus and have loving relationships with others.

Simple organizational efficiency can be achieved through a harnessing of the compulsion to get things done. The problem is efficiency is about all you get. A *godly* organizational efficiency can be achieved with a focus on God and the ensuing outflow of connection with our fellow man. In a godly efficiency, tasks are completed AND relationships are strengthened. With the inevitable high tide coming, I would like relationship with a nice sand castle on the side instead of sitting alone watching the waves lap the walls of my mammoth sand castle.

Many of us Christians assume that our church and our minds are immune to the achiever or busybody mentality. We have been born again and our churches are Bible believing. We talk about having a personal relationship with Jesus. We may even be trying to match our lives to the teaching of scripture. All these things do not mean, however, that we have kicked the habit, the habit to do.

I call it a habit because what happens on the inside is more than a simple cognition. When doers "do" they are getting their fix. There is a certain rush to having a goal, a climax in mind, and working towards that end. There is a rush when one nears goal completion, the culmination of effort, and then is able to rest in the satisfaction of achievement. Achievers go for the big high or the ultimate rush. They will put off little fixes to achieve their grand plan that will bring the ultimate high. Busybodies are more about the daily fix, a constant string of little highs. The high is partially from chemicals in the brain that produce the rush. In part, doers are addicted to the adrenaline. We will discuss the chemical rush from performing tasks in the next chapter. Doers also get a rush from the esteem that task completion brings. Whenever a person completes a task he/she is now competent in that area—in his/her own eyes and in the eyes of his/her peers. People love to be esteemed and being esteemed brings another kind of high. We will address that high in part three of this book. Suffice it now to say that the high is a social high more than a chemical high, but it is as addictive as any drug.

When I gave my life to Christ, I still needed my fix, but instead of performing secular tasks to achieve my rush I would do the work of the ministry. I really didn't think about why I was always busy with a ministry task or why I felt uneasy when I wasn't busy. I just assumed that because I was doing "God's work" that I was where I needed to be. When ministry becomes compulsive, it can be just as distracting to hearing God's voice as a secular endeavor. I was so busy preaching the word, reaching the lost, and planning programs that I couldn't hear God's voice. Can you guess what God did in His grace and love towards me? That's correct, He gave me another "time out." In this "time out" God let me see myself a little more clearly than before. What I saw was someone who needed the rush of performing tasks.

Questions to Ponder

What actions in your life show that you prefer tasks over you relationship with: God? Your spouse? Your children? Your friends, neighbors, or fellow church members?

Are you a "busybody" or an "achiever"? Would your spouse or close friend agree with this assessment?

How could you use your busybody or achiever mentality in positive, relationship—enhancing ways?

Have you ever been in an organization where people use one another to achieve goals? How did that affect you and the organization?

The Chemical Rush
– Addicted to Doing

We are fearfully and wonderfully made. God has made our bodies so that we can survive and thrive in this world. But humans have a knack for turning things meant for good into something harmful. Just a few examples of turning the good into bad: sex, fire, gunpowder, nuclear energy, and fast food. We have been given a wonderful brain with all sorts of chemicals that help us thrive in our environment. When there is danger or something larger than ourselves that must be accomplished, our brains give us a nice shot of adrenaline to give us a boost in this important situation. It is like Popeye on spinach, but to a lesser degree. We feel strong and confident and say, "Bring it on, Brutus!" We enjoy feeling strong. We like when our hearts race. We enjoy it so much that we seek out situations that will produce this rush. Teenagers play chicken with Mack trucks. Day traders play the stock market. Senior citizens play bingo. In all these situations there is uncertainty or danger in losing something valuable. Like a well-oiled machine, the body senses this uncertainty and gives us adrenaline. We feel alive.

People can seek the adrenaline rush in ways that are looked down on: gambling, racing trains, etc. or in ways that are actually encouraged by our society. Doing job-oriented tasks, playing sports, and building stuff are all endorsed by our culture. The Bible agrees that it is good to perform on the job, exercise, and make things. The danger is when we do these things for the sake of getting a rush. If we work for the rush then we are no different in principle than a compulsive gambler or a daredevil. When "doing" becomes compulsive in this way it leads to burnout and strained relationships with those close to us (God included).

I know what you're thinking, "C'mon, what real harm can come from getting a charge out of doing stuff that is good?" Well, I hope I have emphasized the fact that compulsively doing stuff can distract us from hearing God's voice. That distraction itself is a great tragedy. But we are fooling ourselves, perhaps justifying our actions, if we think that being addicted to the performance rush doesn't hurt our other relationships.

I have recently realized that one of the reasons I like to play team sports is for the rush. I live in a rural area and many men play in softball and basketball leagues. Some of these men literally spend four or five nights a week playing sports. They arrange their lives around the game. Some of their wives (girlfriends actually, marriage isn't considered necessary in these circles) see their husbands less than the teammates. Most of the men have kids too. But the pull of getting a rush causes them to rationalize playing so much. Other men, in more white-collar circles, rationalize their long nights at the office for the same reason. They claim they are trying to provide for the family or keeping the boss happy, but they really stay for the rush of achievement. I once looked down on these compulsive doers, thinking, "Where are their priorities?" Now I realize I am one of those doers. I assumed I liked to play sports for the exercise and for the chance to meet unbelievers. The real reason was that I wanted the rush. How else can I explain the anticipation that I felt the day of a game or how much I thought about playing? If I honestly looked at my thought life I had to admit that sometimes my thoughts about playing equaled my thoughts about God or family. In my head, I knew how ridiculous this was. But my heart was pulled toward the rush whether I admitted it or not. I have learned that whenever tasks occupy my mind more than relationships, a red flag should go up.

God revealed my need for the chemical rush through a particularly bad softball season. I am usually a centerfielder and for the few years prior to this season I was one of the best fielders in the league I played in. I was trying out a new league so no one knew how I played. For some reason, maybe it was my new glove or a spiritual thing, I was horrible in the field the first few games. Because I was so bad the coach didn't want to play me. He would put me in only for a couple of innings because he was afraid I would mess up. After a few games my play improved, but my playing time didn't. The roster was pretty much set based on the first few games. I would fume on the days after a game, thinking about how I could improve: wondering if I would get back to my old level, if I would get more playing time. After a while, I stopped making errors and the other players caught up to the amount I had at the beginning. But I suspected the coach didn't like me because I received so little playing time. I found myself not liking the coach very much. Why? Why did I care so much if I played or didn't play this silly game? Why did I start harboring ill feelings against the coach? Because he kept me from my rush. It was that simple. I knew it was just a silly game and that I should be a servant, but my guts wanted the rush. My relationship with the coach, a man who needed Jesus, was hurt because he was keeping me from my fix. I call this the "fiending begets fiend" phenomenon. When an addict really wants his fix, he/she is said to be "fiending." If someone gets in the way of the addict getting his fix, that person is seen as evil, or as a "fiend" to that addict. The interference could be accidental or innocent but in the addicts mind this person is a fiend of the worst sort.

I wonder how many people have a strained relationship with a co-worker, friend or relative because that person is getting in the way of a fix. I have seen my need to do adversely affect my marriage. I have always wanted to move out of the small town I live in and go do big and important ministries. But ever since the beginning of our marriage, my wife has been reluctant to move. One cause of Wendi's reluctance is her mother, who became very ill a few years into our marriage. Wendi's mother lives next door to us and we help take care of her. About the same time, my stepson's father left his wife for another woman—again. My stepson was just beginning middle school *and* puberty and didn't need even more upheaval in his life. Because of these factors, I knew that Wendi's reluctance to move was justified and staying put was the right course of action. Although I didn't know it at the time, it was also God's way of setting up a "time out" for me. In my head, I knew that God did not want us to move at this time. In my gut, I was seething at not being able to go do bigger and more important ministries that I had gone to seminary for. In my gut, I blamed Wendi for getting in the way of my fix. I had to battle feelings of bitterness and anger because I felt like she was holding me back. Sometimes these feelings would be projected unto my stepson. Fiending begets fiend.

Many family member and friends become a fiend for getting in the way of a fix. When we yell at our kids because we are trying to get something done, I wonder if it is because they are misbehaving or because they are getting in the way of our rush. When we are about to complete a task we get myopic. All we can see is the end and we anticipate that satisfied feeling of completion — then the kids interrupt. Jesus didn't have this problem. He always seized the opportunity to build relationships, even if it meant putting off tasks. In Matthew, chapter 19, we read that Jesus was very busy. He had just arrived in Judea and large crowds came out to hear Him teach and to be healed. In addition to all the people wanting His attention, the religious leaders came out to try to catch Him in some sort of misstatement. In the middle of it all, some people brought their children to be blessed by Jesus. The scripture says, "The disciples rebuked them." The disciples may have thought, "Are you crazy? Don't you see how much we have to complete? The master has more important things to do."

Isn't that how we treat our children and our relationships in general? We see all that we have to finish and the thought of connecting with someone to bless them seems like a waste of precious time and a waste of a good fix. The disciples may have been thinking, "We just outflanked some of our critics who were trying to discredit us. We are about to meet the deadline and finish this pile of work (the crowd). We are on the verge of feeling that satisfied glow of having conquered a big task and now you bring these kids around to distract us?"

Some of the disciples may have been frustrated with the delay in getting the achievement fix, but Jesus was not. He saw the interruption as an opportunity. He saw an opportunity to connect with malleable young souls and their parents. He sensed the opportunity to teach His disciples the value of being like dependent children just wanting attention from the Father. The children were not fiends in the way of a fix. The only thing that Jesus "fiended" for was to be in connection with His Father and inviting a lost world into relationship with God. That is why in the midst of a mountain of tasks; Jesus would connect with people one on one. Look at the story of Zacheus, the Samaritan woman, the woman with the unclean blood flow, these children, and others. In each of these instances Jesus stepped back from His tasks to connect with someone in a personal relationship. The disciples themselves were often twelve big distractions that needed Jesus' constant attention. Jesus poured His life into these twelve in real relationship because He knew that one day the Holy Spirit would empower the disciples to do the same to others. For Jesus, none of these people were fiends getting in the way of His fix. These people were opportunities to spread God's offer of relationship to an estranged world. What Jesus offered, He possessed. He was in close relationship with His Heavenly Father and the Father is where Jesus went to get His fix. The only thing that Jesus needed was connection with the Father. He did not have a compulsive desire to do things. Whatever Jesus did was an outflow of His relationship with God. In the Gospel of John, Jesus says,

"Truly, truly, I say to you, the Son can do nothing of Himself, unless it is something He sees the Father doing; for whatever the Father does, these things the Son also does in like manner. For the Father loves the Son, and shows Him all things that He Himself is doing; and the Father will show Him greater works than these, so that you will marvel." (5:19-20)

Jesus' connection was so close that Jesus did the things that His Father did. No compulsion. The Father loved Jesus and showed Him what He needed to do. Doing was the outflow of relationships and Jesus' doing served His relationships.

This connection with God was the only thing that Jesus felt a deep down compulsion to do. The Gospel of Luke provides this example, "But the news about Him was spreading even farther, and large crowds were gathering to hear Him and to be healed of their sicknesses. *But Jesus Himself would often slip away to the wilderness and pray*". (5:15-16) With every person in the crowd came another task. This one needed healing, this one needed an exorcism, that one needed to repent.

Through it all, Jesus never let the tasks get in the way of his relationship with God. God never had to give Jesus a "time out." Jesus would take the time he needed to connect with God because hearing the Father's voice was his top priority. This loving connection with the Father enabled Jesus to lovingly connect with people.

Jesus invited people who were merely interested in religious tasks into relationship. In John 6: 26-34, Jesus was trying to draw the crowd's attention away from His miracles and towards God. The crowd was interested in the tasks and "tricks" that Jesus performed, especially the miracle of multiplying the loaves. Jesus said, "Do not work for the food which perishes, but for the food which endures to eternal life, which the Son of Man will give to you, for on Him the Father, God, has set His seal." The crowd responded, "What shall we do, so that we may work the works of God?" Jesus managed to get the crowd's mind off of His miracles, but instead of focusing on eternal things, they began wondering what tasks, or work, they should do. Not ready to give up on the crowd Jesus answered, "This is the work of God, that you believe in Him whom He has sent." Jesus was explaining that what God wanted from them wasn't ritual or task completion—God wanted them to have a faith relationship to His Son.

Today we are in a crowd very similar to the crowd Jesus spoke to. We are so focused on doing things for the rush that we lose sight of the relationship that God is calling us to in Jesus. Our motivations become so driven by the rush that instead of loving our family and neighbors, we see them as a nuisance.

Are we so addicted to the rush of doing things that our relationships take a back seat? If so, God may give us a "time out" and pull back the curtain of our motivations so that our relationships will once again thrive.

Questions to Ponder

When you aren't doing anything, do you have withdrawal symptoms such as restlessness, depression, irritability and trouble sleeping?

Can you remember any instances in your life when your need to accomplish certain tasks hurt your relationships—or a time when someone became a "fiend in way of your fix"?

What have you chosen to do recently, and in the past, *because* it gave you a rush?

Do you treat others as opportunities or distractions?

How did Jesus balance accomplishing many tasks while maintaining a strong relationship with God and strong relationships with people?

What concrete steps can you take to approach this Jesus-type of balance?

Part 3
Playing to the Crowd.

The Esteem Rush

Our compulsion to do is not only driven by our quest for an adrenaline rush. We are also esteem-powered engines. Our actions are often chosen and powered by esteem. When we perform at a high-level people take notice and praise us for it. We all prefer commendation to condemnation. This preference is normal and healthy. When we begin to do things to *get* that praise, we start to become compulsive doers. Much like chemical addiction we start choosing what and how much we do based on the esteem rush it will bring. This tendency can be found in abundance in our culture. Why do boys put so much more effort into sports than academics? They receive a larger esteem rush from sports in our culture. Both boys and girls buy clothes based on the esteem it will bring or take away. And if you think you have grown out of looking for the esteem rush why does it bother you so much when your kids act up in the store? Aren't you afraid people may esteem you less as a parent? Most sports and luxury cars are sold to adults because adults like the esteem of having a nice car—as if that has any reflection on them as a person. We may think that the esteem rush is something for teenagers but it is just as prevalent in adults, adults are simply more discreet. Children, at least, have an excuse. Children are trying to form an identity and are exploring what brings them self esteem and esteem from others. Children are testing to see if what they do has any effect on the people around them. In short, part of the maturing process for kids is to do things to receive esteem from their parents and from others. While a child's need to receive esteem may be compulsive at times, it is a part of the process of developing independence and the confidence to one day live in the adult world. The problem is that many Americans never grow out of this phase. Many Christians are also stuck in this pursuit of esteem. We claim to "fear God and not man," assuming that we don't pursue this esteem rush, but Christians are not immune to the addiction to esteem.

King Saul was a God-fearing Israelite who pursued the esteem rush to such a degree that by the end of his life his relationship with God was in shambles. When Saul was battling the Philistines, Goliath taunted the armies of Israel and the Israelites looked like fools as they ran and hid from the giant. It was a time of impending defeat and shame for the Hebrews. As you probably know, David took Goliath up on his challenge because he knew that God could easily defeat this giant using anyone He wanted. David was victorious and the Philistines fled. Instead of defeat, Israel had a great victory. One would assume that Saul was ecstatic that David saved his kingdom. Saul was actually displeased at the events. 1 Samuel 19:6-9 describes the episode in this way:

"It happened as they were coming, when David returned from killing the Philistine, that the women came out of all the cities of Israel, singing and dancing, to meet King Saul, with tambourines, with joy and with musical instruments. The women sang as they played, and said, 'Saul has slain his thousands, and David his ten-thousands.'

Then Saul became very angry, for this saying displeased him, and he said, "They have ascribed to David ten-thousands, but to me they have ascribed thousands. Now what more can he have but the kingdom?' Saul looked at David with suspicion from that day on."

Saul wanted the esteem rush from his people. When David received more esteem than Saul, Saul saw David as a fiend for cheating him out of his esteem fix. David received the king-sized esteem rush that Saul deserved as king. This episode began a long story of Saul trying to kill David. Instead of being inspired by David's faith in God and rededicating his own life to God, Saul let his desire for esteem separate him farther from God. Remember, Saul is a man who received the Holy Spirit to such a degree that the Israelites once asked, "Is Saul also among the prophets?" (See 1 Samuel 10:11-13) In the beginning Saul heard the voice of God and the Spirit of the Lord came upon him. By the end of his life, however, Saul was so deaf to God's voice that he consulted a witch (1 Sam. 28) in a desperate attempt to reconnect with the supernatural. I am not saying that Saul's need for an esteem rush was the only cause of his downfall. But it is clear that when David killed Goliath and Saul was jealous, Saul missed hearing God's voice because he was so concerned with esteem. This need for esteem caused Saul to act in ways that were not within God's will. That is the issue. It was not God's voice, but Saul's need for an esteem fix, that dictated Saul's actions.

What Saul did on a grand scale, we Christians do in our own way. Our actions do not spring from hearing God's voice but from our thirst for esteem. If this isn't so, how can one explain the following common scenarios: The pastor who doesn't put as much preparation into a sermon because he knows not many people will be in attendance that week. A church member known for evangelism is upset that he has been witnessing to someone for weeks but another member leads them in the sinner's prayer. A coordinator is irate when left out of the "Thanks to…" column in the church bulletin after putting on a large church function.

In the first example, the pastor knows that he won't get as much esteem as usual so his investment of effort is adjusted to match the return on his rush. In the last two instances, someone is being cheated out of esteem. Whoever is responsible for depriving them of their esteem rush is a fiend. This behavior is very similar to Saul's in the biblical case study we looked at above. In all these cases, behavior, attitudes, and judgments are based on the esteem it yields. Again, God desires that our actions flow from our relationships—especially our relationship with God. If God is trying to cultivate an intimate love relationship with us and we are too busy playing to the crowd, we will not hear His voice. Saul was so concerned with the crowd that he became deaf to what God was doing through David. Are we so focused on what people say that we can't hear God's input? This deafness is one of the primary reasons God gives a "time out."

I often have to give my children "time outs" because they become too silly when showing off. They can't hear my voice because their focus is on getting esteem by making people laugh. Invariably, they do something they are not supposed to because pushing the envelope is always good for a laugh. In the end, Abbi or Isaiah did not hear my warnings and their actions were not a result of relationship, but an attempt to gain esteem. That is why Abbi and Isaiah are given a "time out" and that is often why God puts their father (me) in time out too.

Why do we always feel the need to be doing something? Why do we choose to do the particular things we do? As the above examples show, perhaps it is because we want to get that rush of esteem. Instead of our actions being the outflow of a relationship with God, or a love for people, an examination of our motives reveals that we want the rush from being esteemed. In Matthew 6: 1-8, Jesus confronted the human desire to do things to be esteemed by others. He said:

"Beware of practicing your righteousness before men to be noticed by them; otherwise you have no reward with your Father who is in Heaven. So when you give to the poor, do not sound a trumpet before you, as the hypocrites do in the synagogues and in the streets, so that they may be honored by men. Truly I say to you, they have their reward in full. But when you give to the poor, do not let your left hand know what your right hand is doing, so that your giving will be in secret; and your Father who sees what is done in secret will reward you.

When you pray, you are not to be like the hypocrites; for they love to stand and pray in the synagogues and on the street corners so that they may be seen by men. Truly I say to you, they have their reward in full. But you, when you pray, go into your inner room, close your door and pray to your Father who is in secret, and your Father who sees what is done in secret will reward you."

Jesus said that if we do things for esteem that is *all* we receive. Instead of working towards a relationship with God and receiving a God-sized reward, our reward is esteem from people that is based on show and is short-lived. From experience I know that instead of satisfying our desire for esteem, being noticed only makes us want even more esteem. It is like an addict thinking that his cravings will be satisfied when he finally gets a hit. Soon the cravings come back, but this time the addict needs even more drug just to get the same rush as before. When we do things for an esteem rush, we are in the same cycle. We feel good for a time; we believe what people are saying about us—that we are great. But people soon forget and we start wondering if we are still really that great. So we go back to the crack house of esteem. To save us from this bondage, and to save us *to* a relationship with Him, God will give us a "time out." God will do what it takes to hone our ability to hear His voice and live out our love for Him and not our love for esteem.

Questions to Ponder

Do you choose your actions based on the esteem it brings, or based on your perception of God's will? How does your motivation affect how you view that task?

Can you remember a time when you got angry at someone for getting in the way of an esteem rush?

Have you ever adjusted your effort because you knew you would get more or less esteem than planned?

In what ways do you "practice your righteousness before men to be noticed by them"?

How does your desire for esteem adversely affect your relationship with God?

Image is Everything

What we do for esteem depends on what subgroup or culture we belong to. This truth became clear when I attended the Southern Baptist Theological Seminary's extension center outside of Boston. I was required to go to the main campus in Louisville about once a year. At the main campus I noticed many people always took up the most conservative position. They took pride in being esteemed as the most conservative. Many of my peers didn't realize that what they were saying and doing was a knee jerk reaction to keep up their image. For a time, I looked down on my peers for seeking the esteem of men. I wasn't so haughty when God convicted me of engaging in the same esteem seeking in a different way. Being from New England I live in a bastion of liberalism and many of my neighbors consider me a conservative. Down South, however, and especially in Seminary I took pride in being on the "cutting edge." I thought these hicks from the Bible Belt were stuck in their unbiblical traditions while I was living in a cutting edge mission area. I always spoke up for considering people who aren't from a Christian culture and for reaching the lost. I made sure everyone knew that is what *I* had to do in ministry. Whether I was right or wrong was not the issue. The issue was I acted a certain way to keep up an image. I liked advertising myself as a cutting edge church planter in a mission field. This image brought me esteem from the subculture that I valued most. I realized that some of the classes I took, and the ministry tasks I chose, were based on keeping the cutting edge image that brought me the rush of esteem from my peers.

We usually end up internalizing the standards of esteem that we receive from our peers. When we perform at a high level not only do we receive the chemical rush spoken about in the last chapter, we get a shot of esteem. I hesitate to call it "self-esteem" because the values are not our own but borrowed. Our esteem isn't derived from our relationships but from performing. If we perform a certain set of actions that would bring esteem from our peers (whether they are present or not), we feel a rush knowing we are one of the "most": The one who reads the Bible the most. The one who tithes the most. The one who knows the most about sports, or prophecy, or evangelism. Even if we are not in a literal crowd like the hypocritical Pharisees Jesus was talking about in Matthew 6, we play to a crowd in our mind. We have a crowd of values that we collect from the people around us and we know what makes them cheer. Even if there is not a literal person to see how much we pray, the crowd in our mind lets us know that we pray more than most and we deserve acclaim.

In our thoughts we also play to this crowd in our mind. As Brennon Manning points out in *The Ragamuffin Gospel*[4], we use up our imagination on ourselves instead of God. God has given humans a great imagination to see with the mind what the eye cannot see. Instead of imagining God empowering us and making us into neon signs towards God, or God so glorifying himself in the world around us that people are bowled over—we imagine ourselves riding in to save the day and the crowd in our mind enters in to sing our praises. Instead of using our imagination to surf on the unfathomable glory of God, we use it to wallow in the sickening, sticky sweetness of self-glorification. The more our imagination plays these images, the more we internalize what we must do to make the crowd in our mind esteem us. We start valuing, desiring to do, and doing those things that give us the esteem rush. The rush may be greater when literal people are there, but we also get an internal rush from the crowd in our mind. We imagine that we are "one of the most" and now that we have done ____ (fill in the blank), the crowd (literal or in our heads) confirms that we are indeed "the most." Whatever crowd we are performing for drowns out the voice of God. When we can't hear God, He may pull us away to hear His voice.

Perhaps you can't relate to trying to be esteemed as one of "the most." Many people don't concern themselves with being Mr./ Ms. Most because they simply want to meet expectations. Performing to expectations is still seeking performance-based esteem but meeting these expectations doesn't *give* an esteem rush as much as *prevent* an esteem withdrawal. It's as if the health of our self-image is on a constant intravenous drip and as long as we meet expectations our self-image remains alive. When we live this way we choose to do things to maintain the drip instead of maintaining closeness with God. As long as we meet expectations, the I.V. keeps dripping to keep our esteem up. When expectations and self-image are not of God, we start to choose what we do based on passing the expectation. Obviously, these choices mean we are not living by the voice of God and our relationship with God suffers. Instead of living by God's voice we are living by the voice of the expectations. These expectations can come from parents, a spouse, other family members, co-workers, or friends and can stay with a person for decades. I knew a couple of young men who were going into ministry who struggled with a parent's expectation that they "make something of themselves." Of course, the parent and grown child both understood the unsaid implication that success entails making a lot of money and becoming independent. Many times ministry requires raising financial support and these young men were very uncomfortable with being dependant on charitable "hand-outs" because they were not measuring up to the parental expectation. I am pleased to say that these young men looked to fulfill God's expectation of depending on God instead of their earthly parents' expectation that they make something of themselves. When these men looked to God for their self-image and expectations they grew closer to God. Both men are now making an impact in their world as they live out the expectations and identity of beloved children of God.

Unfortunately there are countless instances when earthly expectations have caused a great many people to turn a deaf ear to God so that a delicate self-image would keep receiving its intravenous esteem drip. I know a pastor who ran himself ragged trying to meet the expectations of the church's board of deacons. Although the pastor worked very hard, he was dismissed in a few years. My friend ended up being miserable, over-worked, and ineffective. Although he meant well, his desire to meet expectations made him stray from the source of his strength, the source of his identity as a beloved child of God.

Whether we strive for a super shot of esteem, or just strive to meet expectations, the performance-based esteem breeds what Brent Curtis and John Eldridge[5] call "false selves." In their book, *The Sacred Romance*, they write, "Think about the part you find yourself playing, the self you put on like a costume. Who cast you in this role? Most of us are living out a script that someone else has written for us. We've not been invited to live from our heart, to be who we truly are, so we put on these false selves hoping to offer something more acceptable to the world, something functional." I think the term "false self" is very appropriate because we so internalize the value judgments of our peers. We know that performing certain tasks or maintaining a certain image will bring us the esteem we desire. So we internally change our desires, our values, to match what others think. In our head we actually start desiring to do this or that, but the desire springs up from our esteem seeking, not our relationships.

For much of my life I have operated on performance-based esteem. Whatever I did, I strived to be the best. I strove to be the funniest and most debaucherous in high school. Those qualities were the most esteemed in my High School peer group, so I did funny and debaucherous things and was very popular for it. In the

Army, I got the highest test scores in my specialty. In college, I got the best grades. Wherever I was, I strived to be one of the best. I would observe the situation and see what things were the most esteemed and that is what I strove for. I did whatever was required in that subculture to fulfill the image of being one of the "most" or best.

When I became a Christian, I knew in my head that what God thought of me was most important. In my gut, however, I still desired to get the performance-based esteem rush from my peers. As a Christian I continued to strive towards those things that made me esteemed as the best. As I went to different churches or ministries, I found that each had its own little subculture. Each group, therefore, also esteemed certain aspects of Christianity more than others. Just as in the former, pre-Christian era of my life, I found that my concept of what I was supposed to do changed with every new input. Of course, I wasn't really aware that I lived this way. In my head, I justified my perfectionism because "Whatever you do, do as unto the Lord." Or "Whatever you do, do in the name of Jesus." Wanting to do my best for God was the right way to live. If I really looked at my motivations, however, I wasn't striving to be the best for God's glory, but my own. My desire to do these spiritual things did not arise from experiencing God. The desires came from my default tendency to try and be the best at everything so I would feel good about myself. The problem was that every time I entered a new subculture, every time I read a book, took a seminary class, or even listened to a sermon—my concept of what I was supposed to do changed slightly. One author stressed the need to know arguments for the faith. So, for a while, I brushed up on that subject, told other people about it, and tried to live it in my life. Another author stressed the need to reach the lost. So for a while, I brushed up on that subject, told other people about it, and tried to live it in my life. This was how I lived. Because these desires weren't necessarily an outflow of my own experience with God, they were false. The desires were a product of my knee jerk reaction to do whatever I am supposed to do. Even if no one else knew about it, I was still getting a performance-based esteem rush because I knew that I was living up to the standards of my subculture.

Do you see how this performance-based esteem breeds false selves? The reason for doing things was not from me, from my spirit, or from my own interaction with God. Doing things was a front, it was a payoff to keep up the image and get the esteem. The image wasn't really me; it was as *The Sacred Romance* pointed out a "false self hoping to offer something more acceptable to the world, something functional."[6] Engaging in certain activities was a payoff for the drug of esteem. The pragmatists may say, "What does it matter as long as you prayed more, evangelized more, etc., etc.?" It matters a great deal. God wants our hearts and a relationship with us. Praying, evangelizing, and all the other "religious" acts are not ends in themselves. Our actions should be a result of, or a striving towards, a relationship with God. When we live for esteem, it becomes more and more difficult to know what the crowd in our mind is saying versus what the Heavenly Father is saying. If we are listening to the roar of the crowd we will not be able to discern the still small voice of God and all the joy, power, and fulfillment that comes from His lips. We will be doing Christian stuff, but we will be missing what God brought us into this world for.

The first time God revealed my performance-based false self was towards the end of seminary. As a part of the curriculum I was to meet with a mentor who would help me reach some ministry goals. I had just read John Piper[7] and A.W. Tozer[8] and knew in my head that I should desire to know God above all else. I remember saying to my mentor, John, how I needed to not allow ministry tasks to get in the way of seeking and knowing God. What he said (actually what God said through him) was, "Do you really feel that way, or do you just know that is how you are supposed to feel?" I began to realize that I performed, felt, and desired many things because I was supposed to. Tozer and Piper had instructed me on what I needed to be the most spiritual. Although Tozer and Piper were right, my motivations were wrong. The voice of God, through these authors, was not directing me—the desire to be the "most" was directing my actions. This revelation through my mentor began a long process of God revealing my need to be the best. I do whatever I must do for that rush of esteem. Yes, the esteem often is from within, but the esteem has its origin in what others would highly regard (the crowd in our minds). The image I tried to live out and the tasks I chose flowed from my need for an esteem fix more than from my relationship with God. I was not guided by the voice of the Father, but by the voice of the crowd in my mind reminding me what I need to do to make them cheer.

The danger of being addicted to the esteem rush, or the chemical rush talked of earlier, is that the addiction muffles our ears to the voice of the Father. We are so busy performing that we ignore the voice of the Father calling us to know Him. His invitation is for us to sit on His lap so that we grow into the Christ-like children He created us to be. If we continue to reject this invitation, God in His grace, may give us a "time out." In "time out," with no crowd to please and all other options closed, we can put away the show and finally run into the Heavenly Father's embrace.

Questions to Ponder

What image are you most concerned with maintaining?

In the different subcultures you live in, what tasks are esteemed the most? What are you "supposed to" be doing in each subculture? Do you find yourself acting differently in different situation in response to esteem?

What makes the crowd in your mind cheer the most? What makes them jeer?

In what ways do you present a "false self" to the world?

Think of a time when your actions were based on hearing God's voice. Compare that to a time when you chose a task based on keeping up an image. How did the different motivations affect how you felt and how you carried out that task? How did the different motivations affect your relationship with God and with your peers?

Performance Churches

There are whole churches, even denominations, which function primarily out of a performance-based esteem model. I have witnessed this model at work in varying degrees in many church settings.

Earlier I had mentioned my first "time out." God had been trying to draw me closer to Himself and away from my grand plan for some time. I couldn't hear Him because I was so busy doing big and esteem-worthy things. God brought about my first "time out" through an interaction with a Bible cult. God knew that I was in a thick daze and needed a hard slap. My extreme deafness prompted God to send this group of in-your-face, performance-based esteem (and salvation), control freaks into my life. They really spoke my language. I was impressed that almost all the members seemed to be really driven to serve God. Thanks to their persistence I started to study the Bible with them and on my own. As I read the Bible and once again felt God's pull on me, I knew that God was the only thing worth living for. My grand, seven-year plan would lead me to meaninglessness. God would lead me to real, everlasting meaning. As I realized my need for God, the cult tried to make me realize my need to perform. Again, this really spoke to my disposition. The culture of the cult also spoke to my disposition. People who gave the most and converted the most people were esteemed the most—big time. People who didn't perform were castigated and members considered them spiritually weak. Performance based esteem fueled the engine of this hard-working, albeit controlling, church culture.

Daren was the first member I met. He was a handsome African American college student and a new convert who had a background with the Pentecostal church. After a couple meetings, a "higher ranking" Asian man started meeting with me. After I was a member of the group I learned that this switch took place because the cult didn't want to trust my conversion to a new convert. After all, they had been looking for a "sharp looking white guy" to convert for some time. The leaders understood that in order to convert more white people, they needed more white people (Mainline churches call this the homogeneous unit principle). The esteem of this section of the cult depended on more converts, and in their efforts to control performance they didn't let Daren handle this sharp looking white guy. I remember Daren telling me that he was angry that he didn't get to disciple me. He was angry, as I see it now, because he was cheated out of the esteem fix that he would receive for getting another disciple notch on his belt. The leaders, however, were also fiending on the performance rush and they didn't want to take any chances in losing this opportunity to get a steady source of esteem as this sharp looking white guy brought in other sharp looking white guys.

The need for control is a hallmark of performance-based esteem, but so is frustration. When self-esteem is based on others' assessment of your performance, you desperately want to control the situation. You want to stack the deck as much as possible so that the outcome will be more sure. Your rush and your feeling of self-worth depend on positive results. Inevitably, all outcomes can't be controlled and despite all the effort, you enter a period when everything seems to go wrong. You work harder and harder to feel good. Eventually you burn out. This burn out can also result from success, because the more esteem you receive the more you crave. After success, you must do even more to outdo your last performance. Over time, the expectations from without and within become too much and you become frustrated and burnt out.

I did not stay in the Bible cult long enough to burn out. But now that I am out and have researched this cult (the International Church of Christ, a.k.a. the I.C.C. or the Boston Church of Christ) it appears that they lose about the same number of members as they gain. Most of the people who leave the ICC say they left because of burnout. When a church tries to control members by using performance esteem, people eventually are worn down to emptiness. In contrast, when members are freed to listen to God and respond to His voice, they grow in joy *and* energy.

You may think that because your church is not a cult then it doesn't have problems with performance-based esteem. I hope this is the case, but Satan often tries to introduce performance-based esteem into a church body to keep it ineffective and pacified on performing for a rush. What Satan does not want is a body to be in close connection with God so that everything in the body is the efflux of a love relationship with the Father.

Performance-based esteem exists in differing amounts depending on the church. The system thrives when there are certain people in the church who are considered the most spiritual because they perform all the tasks that the particular church esteems. I have been in churches where prophesy and apologetics are considered the highest attainments so the leading men make sure they have all their end times books and Josh McDowell (a leading apologist) at the ready. Other churches hold up evangelists the most. In some Pentecostal churches you must speak in tongues if you want to be considered spiritual. People sitting in the pew quickly figure the system out. They need to perform if they want any esteem. Across America there are Christians trying to win the most souls, others pretending to speak in tongues, and others acting as if end times prophesy actually intrigued them. For what? For a shot of the esteem. And the leaders of the church perpetuate the system because members are doing more of what they want. They think, "Who cares why people are doing more of what I want as long as they are doing it?" God cares. Proverbs 16:2 reads, "All the ways of a man are clean in his own sight, but the Lord weighs the motives." We assume that because offerings, attendance, and sermon tape sales are up the church must be doing something right. Maybe and maybe not. Perhaps parishioners are trying to be the "most": the most faithful attendee, the largest giver (so they can be listed under the "faithful sustainers" category in the annual report) or the one who speaks in tongues the most. Everything may seem clean, but God, who weighs the motives, sees a church of junkies who are competing for the biggest rush. God also sees that the church leaders are the pushers who keep the status quo so that they can get their own fix for having the church that is most _____ (fill in the blank).

In a performance-based esteem system there is usually a lot of judging. Some of the judging is subtle, some not so subtle. There is a self-policing mechanism within the church and the punishments and rewards have to do with the taking away or giving of esteem. If someone is to be judged as very (or better still, "most") spiritual then they must comply with certain "to do" and "not to do" lists. Of course these are not literal lists, but everyone in the church is soon conditioned to know what is on the lists. Like Pavlovian dogs we do something and we are rewarded not with a biscuit, but with esteem. There really isn't much room for diversity of worship or scriptural understanding in these cases. There may be talk of freedom but in reality this is a police state. Sure, you don't *have to* do all these things, but if you don't you can expect to be judged as not ready or in need of more understanding and further growth before you can be a decision maker in the church. Works can be a gauge of one's faith, but only when works flow from faith. When we gauge spiritual deeds by cultural preferences instead of the Word of God we value performance over love.

In contrast to a church that runs by esteem, a healthy church fosters a genuine thirst for God. Certain activities are encouraged or discouraged not based on esteem, but based on that activity's value in knowing God and living the life that God intended. A healthy church also recognizes that God has given many gifts, personalities, and talents. All this diversity is equally esteemed within the body since what one does is less important than one's thirst to know God. When there is a genuine thirst to know God more, people will do those things that help them attain that goal.

Questions to Ponder

Performance-based esteem is the norm among the secular culture. In what ways does this model creep into the church?

Have you ever been in a situation where esteem was used to control people?

What spiritual tasks do you currently feel pressured to perform based on the performance-based esteem model?

Managing Esteem Instead
of Performance—Social Proof

Performing for esteem can be very draining. There is another (equally draining) way to cope in a performance-based esteem system. Instead of just altering what is done (performance), one can work on the other side of the equation (esteem). If a certain group is not giving esteem for performance one can carve out or gather a new group that will. This is a rather normal human action—" birds of a feather flock together" goes the saying. People who think and act like we do always give us more esteem than people who don't. In fact, people who are not like us can really challenge our self- esteem if we are caught in the performance-based esteem model. Instead of our thoughts, actions, or beliefs bringing affirmation by someone who agrees that we are right, our thoughts, actions, or beliefs are questioned. This dissonance is an esteem anti-rush or downer. We don't like people who bring us down, so we either try to change them or run away from them to a more agreeable person. In either case, we are not allowing an intimate relationship with God to be the steady rock that supports our faith and self-image. We are relying on social proof.

What is "social proof"? Social proof is the affirmation or proof that we receive from people who agree with us. Social proof is the reason we are so interested in polls. If four out of five people prefer peanuts to walnuts, then this is proof that peanuts are better. I happen to like walnuts, so despite the fact that the prevailing social proof in society is pro-peanut, I can convince myself that walnuts are better if I just surround myself with the 20% of the population who likes walnuts. In my walnut subculture I receive plenty of performance-(in this case my liking for walnuts) based esteem and affirmation that I am right.

Instead of withdrawing into the walnut subculture, I could take another approach. I could seek to convert people to liking walnuts. I could always make sure I had a dish of walnuts on my desk at work so people could try them. I could wear T-shirts that declare the supremacy of the walnut. At the work place and marketplace I could argue that peanuts are not really nuts at all—they are legumes. With every walnut convert I receive social proof that my position is right. If someone is so convinced that they switch from peanuts to walnuts then I must be right!

With this silly example I am by no means suggesting that our belief in God is simply a matter of personal taste. I am arguing that our actions can convey that message when our motivation for sharing our faith is more about a need for social proof than a need to do the will of the Father. When we are doing, thinking, or saying things because we desire social proof, people tend to discern that. You can probably discern the difference between someone who has to be right as opposed to someone who is genuinely seeking truth. The person who needs to be right will not allow for disagreement or challenge to their position, it is too hurtful to their self-image. A person reacts this way because their position has not been arrived at through an honest seeking of truth, but by an accumulation of social proof. Unfortunately, this reaction also exists in some Christians. If someone's family and social group all believe in Jesus, it is possible that a person "believes" because of the social proof and not because they have actually encountered the living God. When that person's faith is challenged they usually lash out and try to use deceptive arguments in order to win the discussion and feel right. Unfortunately, this is why many non-believers think of Christians as ignorant and hypocritical.

In Christianity, many people need a "time out" because they are doing things as a result of social proof instead of the voice of the Father. This need for social proof doesn't just impact evangelism; it is one of the great causes of church splits. As Christians, our commonality in Christ is supposed to supercede all differences. Galatians 3:26-28 says:

"For you are all sons of God through faith in Christ Jesus. For all of you who were baptized into Christ have clothed yourselves with Christ. There is neither Jew nor Greek, there is neither slave nor free man, there is neither male nor female; for you are all one in Christ Jesus."

Our commonality in Christ makes all of our differences seem insignificant. In contrast, esteem seeking through social proof demands that differences be changed or withdrawn from. Lack of social proof is too much of a drain on our esteem.

I first learned about social proof in a social psychology class. Certain apocalyptic cults have become case studies for social proof. One particular cult proclaimed that the world would be destroyed on a certain day. The cult was fairly reclusive, but did warn a few people about the upcoming apocalypse. When the day for the world to end came—and went—a strange thing happened. Instead of disbanding, saying, "Oops" and returning to society, the cult members started evangelizing! The cult prophet received a new message explaining why the world didn't end and instructions to go tell the world this new message.

This pattern of apocalyptic misses followed by an increase in evangelism is not uncommon. The theory is that in the face of proof that challenges our deeply held beliefs (in this case the proof that the world didn't end when predicted) we will turn to social proof to anchor our beliefs. When measurable evidence indicates our beliefs are misguided, we try to convert people. We reason that if people convert there must be more to our beliefs than the proof suggests.

If you are not a member of an apocalyptic cult, you may still employ social proof. There are many Christians, Jehovah's witnesses, and Mormons who do evangelism based more on their lack of faith, than their faith. Subconsciously they feel compelled to convert people because it makes them feel more sure about their faith. Biblical evangelism, however, is an outflow of one's love relationship with God.

The so-called, "holy huddle" is also an expression of social proof. The holy huddle is when a church isolates itself from the world so that it can beat its drum unquestioned. Without outside ideas everyone can be 100% convinced since there is 100% agreement in this little subculture. In contrast, Biblical faith penetrates the surrounding culture and in the midst of questions, contempt, and persecution, the faith remains strong. Biblical faith is resolute because it is based on a relationship with God and not popular opinion.

For most Christians this reliance on social proof exhibits itself mostly as a feeling in response to disagreement. This disagreement can come either from a skeptic, or just a fellow believer with some doctrinal differences. In either case we get that feeling to go on the offensive. The feeling is not based on truth or love for that other person. It is an uneasy feeling that we are wrong. When our beliefs are more grounded in social proof than in a relationship with God, we are more prone to be uneasy with disagreement because it is social proof in the other direction. I am not speaking about valid arguments that prompt us to revisit an issue to make sure we have it straight—that is healthy and open minded. I have in mind the gut reaction to disagreement itself, regardless of the content. This gut feeling, if acted upon, compels us to argue in a way to defeat a person more than guide them. This feeling causes people in the church to take up sides as the disagreeing people scurry to shore up some social proof from within the church. This feeling causes us to be cold to people who are different in the church because we are uncomfortable with the social proof against us.

We don't like being uncomfortable; we don't like being deprived of our esteem rush from those who disagree. Our seeking of social proof, and the pleasure that goes with it, causes many rifts in the church. James, in his epistle, wrote:

> "What is the source of quarrels and conflicts among you? Is not the source your pleasures that wage war in your members? You lust and do not have; so you commit murder. You are envious and cannot obtain; so you fight and quarrel. You do not have because you do not ask. You ask and do not receive, because you ask with wrong motives, so that you may spend it on your pleasures. . . . Draw near to God and He will draw near to you. Cleanse your hands, you sinners; and purify your hearts, you double-minded." (4:1-8)

The principles in the letter of James apply to the rifts that develop as a result of our need for esteem. The source of these quarrels is our pleasures: the pleasure we receive from esteem. When we don't receive esteem, we gather people that agree with us and bolster our social proof. Of course, those who disagree do the same and then rifts develop in the church. But the source of the rifts is our need for pleasure. We need to feel good about ourselves and if our beliefs are based on social proof, then when our social proof is undermined we have that gut reaction to defeat the naysayers. James points out that sometimes we will even ask God to intervene in the affair. But we ask only so that the other person will be shown to be wrong. We "ask with wrong motives, so that we may spend it on our pleasures." We are not really looking for unity, or reconciliation. We are looking for our pleasure to be restored. The irony is that the only way for true pleasure and unity to be restored is to stop seeking pleasure (social proof esteem) and "draw near to God...cleanse hands, and purify hearts." A "time out" to draw near to God is the best way to resolve conflict. We must seek God instead of social proof and our hearts will be purified as we begin to interact with one another in a Christ-like manner. When conflict arises due to seeking the pleasure of social proof we must take a "time out" to draw near to God.

Social proof and performance-based esteem are two sides of the same coin. That coin is the system that is fueled by esteem rush. Choosing to perform certain tasks based on the esteem rush it brings or gathering a group of yes-men to esteem what you already do are both attempts to get an esteem rush. Whenever we choose our actions based on the esteem it brings, we are ignoring the voice of God. We are, in essence, children in a classroom doing silly things to get the attention of our peers. Hopefully, our classroom teachers aren't going to put up with such behavior. (Maybe they will give the kids a "time out" in the principal's office.) Unfortunately, all too many churches are classrooms that teach and acculturate us into the performance-based esteem system.

Questions to Ponder

How does social proof and polling affect the decision making process on an individual, church and societal level?

How comfortable are you in the face of disagreement? Is your knee jerk reaction to defeat those who disagree with you?

What face of social proof are you most familiar with: compulsion to convert, or the "holy huddle"?

How would you describe the differences between a biblical faith and a faith that is based on social proof? Can you think of actual examples from your life?

Have you ever been in a situation where people were in conflict and trying to muster social proof? How did that impact the situation and the relationships involved?

If social proof and performance-based esteem are two sides of the same coin, which side of the coin do you tend towards?

Breaking Free from the Performance Esteem Model

Two things must change in order for American Christianity to break free from the performance esteem system: the individual and the church. As individuals we need to break our habit of needing an esteem fix. Without a demand for any drug, the system that sells the drugs collapses. If there are enough individuals in a church who refuse to be a part of the supply and demand cycle of esteem, the system no longer works. One problem is that we, as individuals, often do things for esteem without even thinking. As has been said, our need for esteem is so deep and pervasive that seeking esteem actually seems more natural than seeking the voice of God. To complicate things even more, scripture tells us to bless people because God wants us to be a source of joy to others. A part of blessing someone is doing things that please him or her. We can't stop trying to make people happy because that would be just as sinful as pleasing people for esteem. God calls us to be in a loving, blessing relationship with other people. How then can we please people to bless them without pleasing people for esteem? A principle that can guide us through these murky waters is found in 1 Corinthians 10:31-33. The apostle Paul wrote:

"Whether, then, you eat or drink or whatever you do, do all to the glory of God. Give no offense either to Jews or to Greeks or to the church of God; just as I also please all men in all things, not seeking my own profit but the profit of the many, so that they may be saved."

Using this principle we can ask ourselves some questions to see if we are acting for performance esteem or for relationship. First, we ask ourselves if we are doing what we are doing "to the glory of God." If there is any smacking of social proof or gaining esteem then we are seeking our own glory—not God's. We also ask ourselves if we are acting in a way that, as much as possible, won't offend people and if we are doing things in a way that will ultimately benefit others. The key is making sure we are not pleasing people for *our* own esteem or "profit" but for *their* happiness and profit. If we undertake a ministry or task and discerned that we truly desire God's glory and the profit of others then we are doing it free of the performance esteem system. This assurance does not preclude us from reevaluating from time to time to make sure that we are still free from the esteem system. Even when we start out right we can drift back into the performance esteem model.

I want to emphasize that ensuring we are living for God's glory and for others' profit does not mean that we ignore our own happiness. When God is glorified and others profit from our tasks, we profit too. We are made happy by our undertakings if we are working within our gifts and calling. When we are functioning within our relationship with God we don't feel compelled to do things just because we are asked. When seeking esteem, however, we take on tasks to receive more esteem. The point is that when we are free from the shackles of esteem seeking there is much profit and joy as tasks actually help our relationships instead of hurt them. In America, we are mistakenly obsessed with self-centered happiness. But true happiness is relationship centered and brings joy to all parties involved.

Confronting yourself with the above questions before taking on a task is just one tool to help you as an individual (there are more of these tools in following chapters) begin to break the performance esteem system that you find yourself in. If you, and other individuals in your church, begin to break the demand for esteem in your church then the performance esteem culture in your church begins to change. This is a bottom up, or grass roots, kind of change.

On the other side, if the system exists in a church, it needs to be addressed on an organizational level as well. This can be done if the leaders of the church refuse to perpetuate the system—a top down kind of change. The apostle Paul addressed the principles that underpin this kind of change in Romans 14.

The context of Paul's writing was a common scenario in the churches he started and a scenario he assumed the Roman church was also dealing with. More and more Gentiles were joining the church. These Gentiles didn't live by Jewish culture and didn't follow many of the ceremonial laws of the Jews. These laws included dietary restrictions and proscriptions concerning festival days. The issue was formally resolved (Acts 15) at the Jerusalem council where the apostles decided that Gentiles didn't need to become Jews before becoming Christians. The Gentiles only needed to follow the moral law of God. The ceremonial law of the Jews that set them apart from the pagan nations was no longer necessary because one only needed faith in Christ to be a Christian. The differences in practices between the Jewish and gentile Christians had the potential to cause a rift in the church if people worked according to performance esteem or social proof. In Romans 14, Paul wrote:

"Now accept the one who is weak in faith, but not for the purpose of passing judgment on his opinions. One person has faith that he may eat all things, but he who is weak eats vegetables only. The one who eats is not to regard with contempt the one who does not eat, and the one who does not eat is not to judge the one who eats, for God has accepted him. *(This is in reference to Jewish dietary laws)* Who are you to judge the servant of another? To his own master he stands or falls; and he will stand, for the Lord is able to make him stand.

One person regards one day above another, another regards every day alike. *(This refers to the Jewish holy and festival days)* Each person must be fully convinced in his own mind. He who observes the day, observes it for the Lord, and he who eats, does so for the Lord, for he gives thanks to God; and he who eats not, for the Lord he does not eat, and gives thanks to God. For not one of us lives for himself, and not one dies for himself; for if we live, we live for the Lord, or if we die, we die for the Lord; therefore whether we live or die, we are the Lord's. For to this end Christ died and lived again, that He might be Lord both of the dead and of the living.

But you, why do you judge your brother? Or you again, why do you regard your brother with contempt? For we will all stand before the judgment seat of God. For it is written,

'As I live, says the Lord, every knee shall bow to Me,

And every tongue shall give praise to God.'

So then each one of us will give an account of himself to God.

Therefore let us not judge one another anymore, but rather determine this—not to put a stumbling block in a brother's way. I know and am convinced in the Lord Jesus that nothing is unclean in itself; but to him who thinks anything to be unclean, to him it is unclean. For if because of food your brother is hurt, you are no longer walking according to love. Do not destroy with your food him for whom Christ died. Therefore do not let what is for you a good thing be spoken of as evil; for the kingdom of God is not eating and drinking, but righteousness and peace and joy in the Holy Spirit. For he who in this way serves Christ is acceptable to God and approved by men. So then we pursue the things which make for peace and the building up of one another. Do not tear down the work of God for the sake of food. All things indeed are clean, but they are evil for the man who eats and gives offense. It is good not to eat meat or to drink wine, or to do anything by which your brother stumbles. The faith which you have, have as your own conviction before God. Happy is he who does not condemn himself in what he approves. But he who doubts is condemned if he eats, because his eating is not from faith; and whatever is not from faith is sin."

The issue here was that the people in the churches weren't comfortable with the differences that Paul discussed. The Jewish Christians continued to follow much of the dietary laws and festivals that they had always followed. The Gentile Christians continued to eat the food they were accustomed to and paid no special attention to Old Testament festivals. The Apostle Paul either saw the potential for, or heard of, performance-based esteem creeping in. The Jewish group was abstaining from foods or celebrating festivals because all the other Jewish Christians were doing it and they didn't want to be esteemed as less spiritual. Likewise, some of the Gentiles who may have actually been Jewish converts first, perhaps agreed with what the Jewish Christians were doing. However, they didn't want to be considered "judaizers" or legalists so they did things to be esteemed by the gentile Christians. In both cases actions were a result of wanting esteem—not a result of a faith interaction with God.

Paul alludes to the corrosive effect of the social proof system as well. He says, "So then we pursue the things which make for peace and the building up of one another. Do not tear down the work of God for the sake of food…it is good not to eat meat or to drink wine, or *to do anything* by which your brother stumbles." There probably was pressure by both the Jewish and Gentile camps to conform. I am sure there were spirited arguments as each side tried to win people to their opinion, and keep the people already on their side in line. The problem was that when they did convince someone to eat or not eat like a Gentile, they were causing that person to stumble. Why? Because that person wasn't doing it out of faith, but out of a response to the pressures of social proof. As Paul points out, "whatever is not from faith is sin."

Whenever we try to use the system of social proof or performance-based esteem to persuade people to do certain things we are sinning and causing others to sin. Our actions and their actions are not fueled by a love relationship with God, but a love of esteem.

How would the apostle Paul's principles contained in Romans 14 look in the present day? How would it work in a church? We have addressed the bottom-up or grass roots level already. Practical advice to break free of the things that make individuals deaf to God is also contained in Part 5. In terms of top-down change, or changing the system itself, the apostle Paul serves as an example for the leaders of a church to follow.

The first step is to be proactive. The apostle Paul was planning to go to Rome, but had never actually been to the church in Rome. He saw the potential conflict and decided to address the performance-based esteem system. If you have any influence in your church, bring the issue aboveboard so it can be addressed. Even if the performance esteem system isn't a problem yet, it will be a lot easier to identify if people know it is out there.

Secondly, be specific. The apostle Paul took this general principle and applied it to specific differences. With the people in your church, identify existing differences within your church. Some common modern day differences are: contemporary worship music vs. hymns, speaking in tongues vs. not, drinking alcohol vs. not drinking, watching R rated movies vs. not, dressing modestly by 1800s standards vs. dressing modestly by today's standards, using the King James version of the Bible vs. using a modern translation, etc. etc. etc. If any of these issues exist in your church, you probably have noticed that whatever view a person holds, that person is convinced that they have the more spiritual view. The trick, as the apostle Paul puts it, is to be "fully convinced in your own mind" and then have this conviction before God. Bolstering conviction with social proof leads to sin. By being proactive and specific, social proof is nipped in the bud on that particular issue. Also, by specifically bringing the issues out, people will realize that this is not just some abstract problem, but a problem that is lurking at the door of the church and the door of every believer's heart.

Third, create a culture of acceptance. I realize in our society this statement can carry some bad connotations. However, the goal must be to spur one another on to a closer relationship with God. This goal requires being comfortable with the fact that different people express their faith in different ways. Look at the way you expressed your faith at different times in your life and you will agree that even within one life, faith can be expressed in different ways. Keeping a person on the road to a closer walk with God is the most important task. If a person is doing something that makes you uneasy, ask yourself if you are addressing the issue because you are uncomfortable, or because you are genuinely interested in that person's spiritual walk. Often under the banner of accountability we try to change people's actions for more social proof. The problem is that you can get people to modify their behavior, even with "real" sin, but what they truly need is to be eternally transformed through a close relationship with God. If a church has a culture of accepting differences in faith expression at different points in a spiritual life, people can open up and be real. We must create a church culture where real struggles and questions are shared. Otherwise, the chief worry is having esteem taken away.

Fourth, foster a "time out" mentality. Truly uphold a church mindset that a relationship with God is more important than doing tasks. All tasks and ministries take a back seat to cultivating one's relationship with God. If one has to choose between taking time out to hear the voice of God and giving up certain church tasks, then every leader in the church should encourage that person to take time out.

The Bible cult I spoke about in the previous chapter is the poster child for the performance-based esteem model. But let us not be fooled. The performance-based esteem model is also alive and well in the more mainstream churches of America, including yours, if you are a pastor and you are trying to have the most _____ church around or if you are a member of a church and you are trying to be the most _____ in your church. Take a "time out" before God gives you one. Seek to make your actions and the actions of your church a result of hearing the voice of the living God. In a house of addicts, someone has to admit they have a problem to get everyone else healthy again. Maybe that person is you.

Questions to Ponder

Do you please people for *your* own esteem or profit, or for *their* happiness and profit?

Does the Romans 14 model of dealing with differences seem possible in the churches you are familiar with?

What are some differences in your faith community that could become a problem? What issues are subject to one's own conscience and what issues are moral issues that require church discipline?

Stop regarding man, whose breath of life is in his nostrils;
*   For why should he be esteemed?* Isaiah 2:22

Part 4
Other Distractions

Sin, Satan, and a Sound Spotlight

You may be wondering how sin and Satan fit into all this. After all, doesn't continuing in sin keep us from hearing the voice of God? Doesn't Satan try to deceive us so we can't hear God's voice? The answer to both of these questions is "Yes." However, many Christians think of sin and Satan in a way that hinders their walk with God, instead of helps it. I am not implying that sin and Satan are unimportant when it comes to hearing the voice of God. Both sin and Satan, unfortunately, hinder our relationship with God. Often God gives us a "time out" to remove the deafening effect that sin and Satan have on our ability to hear God's voice.

There is a movement within Christianity that, I believe, gives Satan too much credit. Satan or his demons are seen as responsible for every difficulty, affliction, or sin that shows itself. In the name of "spiritual warfare" people are telling Satan or his demons to leave such and such an area. People start addressing Satan and telling him to stop doing whatever he is doing. This concept of Satan credits more power to Satan than he has and perhaps is a corrective to the secular society's influence over the church which argues that Satan doesn't even exist. Satan does exist, but he is not all-powerful. He is not God and it is biblically unclear if he can even be in more than one place at a time. Besides, to think that we would be important enough for Satan to personally show up is a bit prideful I think. We are small fry. How he mostly affects us is not through his personal agency, but in a secondary way, usually though the way of the world.

Satan is powerful, but is not omnipresent, so he usually brings his power to bear on kingdoms and dominions. Satan deceives and tempts people into sin by getting a whole culture to buy into a lie. He confuses billions of people by raising up false prophets who mingle just enough of God's truth to make their words seem right. Satan influences a whole populace into thinking that what is right is wrong and what is wrong is right. The Bible tells us that Satan deceives, accuses and lies. These actions have their most damaging effects when they take root into a society or culture itself. Christians are most affected by Satan because we see the results of his handiwork in the way that our culture and world operate. When we buy into these lies (which is easier to do because most people around us have) our relationship with God suffers. While Satan and demons exist, in my opinion, it is a rare occasion when a Christian in America has to deal with them personally. We are having enough trouble dealing with the powers, dominions and kingdoms influenced by Satan. Satan could probably take a vacation and let what he has already done just keep working.

In that rare case when a personal agent of Satan may be present, we certainly shouldn't be talking to it for any length of time. We need God's power through Jesus and if we are telling the demon to do such and such, hasn't the demon at least taken our eye off of God? We only need to worry about drawing closer to God. When we are filled with the Holy Spirit there is no room for demons in our hearts and the light naturally casts out the darkness. No, our focus needs to be on God.

When God shows up through the Holy Spirit, demons flee. More importantly, dominions fall and deeply ingrained satanic mindsets wash away when we draw close to God. Any power of Satan or demon cowers in the light of the awesome power of God. Demons begged Jesus not to destroy them, but send them into a herd of swine. Jesus only paid enough attention to the demons to tell them to leave. Jesus didn't wonder what satanic spirit was over Jerusalem and he didn't rebuke Satan when Satan entered Judas.

When Satan tempted Jesus in the wilderness, Satan focused on tempting Jesus to be self-sufficient and problem focused. "If you are hungry make bread from these stones. If you are to rule the unbelieving world, worship me and the world is yours," reasoned Satan. Jesus' responses to the temptations were always God focused. (See Matthew 4)

In all of Jesus' dealings with the devil and demons, Jesus focused on God. When God told Jesus to heal someone of demonic affliction, He did—but Jesus remained God focused, not problem (Satan) focused. Jesus' mission was to free the world from the bondage of sin in general. This sin includes Satan's personal attacks, the evil influences that find their birth in Satan's activities, and the sin that we hold to with no help from

Satan at all. Jesus came to set us free from this captivity. We no longer should focus on the prison, but the freedom and the freedom giver. I have heard too may people talking to demons or Satan when they should be talking to God.

Satan hinders our relationship with God. He places lies and accusations all over society to tempt us into turning a deaf ear to God. If we begin to fall victim to Satan's influences (secondary or direct) God may give us a "time out" to focus on the voice of our Heavenly Father. Our Father wants us to be able to discern between His voice and the voice of the stranger. The best way to know God's voice is by becoming so familiar with it that you can pick it out of a babbling crowd.

SIN

Christians often think of sin in a way that hinders them from overcoming sin, as well as hearing God's voice. When we hear the word "sin" we usually think of a particular act (usually sexual) that goes against God. In the Bible, sin has a broader definition. Sin may refer to aiming to do right, but falling short. Sin may be described as a "transgression," connoting a violation of God's laws or commands. When the word "iniquity" is used to describe sin, an inner, sinful disposition is usually in view. In contrast to this biblical view of sin, the popular view of sin tends to be restricted to "transgressions."

Holding to the limited definition of sin effects how we live. God doesn't seem to be in our lives, so we start examining ourselves for something that we have done or not done. We come to the conclusion that we lust after a co-worker, or we lost our temper during the morning commute, or we lied. We ask for forgiveness and then try to stop. The problem with this approach is that it puts the problem of our sin in a tidy little box, it makes us focus on the sin instead of God, and it is not very useful for habitual or deeply engrained sin.

Do not misunderstand me, when there is a sin in your life that you can identify you should ask for forgiveness and not do it again. The Bible says, "Our sins have separated us from our God." (Isaiah 59:2) Our sins cause a wall to go up and God's voice is muffled through that wall. When possible, we should confess it and forget it. The sins that really get us, however, do not go away so easily. We confess the action, only to do the same act a week later. The action is only a symptom of a deeper sin. Sin, in general, doesn't fit into a tidy box. Instead, we have sinful attitudes, priorities and thoughts, which bring about a sinful action. We may confess the particular action, but still be under the sway of iniquity in our thoughts and minds. We assume that because we identified four actions that were sinful and confessed all four actions then the score is zero and we are sin free. When we think of sin in this "scoreboard" sense we don't open ourselves up to God's deep transforming power but we do open ourselves up to hypocrisy. We are free from certain actions and assume that we are where we need to be. The Pharisees had much the same assumption. The Pharisees followed a checklist of particular actions to do or not do. Because the checklist was filled out, the Pharisees saw themselves as more right with God than those who did not follow such a checklist. Jesus said this to them:

"Woe to you, scribes and Pharisees, hypocrites! For you are like whitewashed tombs which on the outside appear beautiful, but inside they are full of dead men's bones and all uncleanness. So you, too, outwardly appear righteous to men, but inwardly you are full of hypocrisy and lawlessness." (Matthew 23:27-28)

We can become like the Pharisees when we think of sin only as a particular action. We may have all the external actions correct, but still have the cancer of sin on the inside. Yes, sin does get in the way of our relationship with God. We are in trouble, however, if we assume we are sin free just because we didn't murder, lie, or commit adultery. The premise of this book is that our actions are often a result of trying to get an adrenaline rush, esteem rush, or a result of something other than faith in God. These motivations are subtle, internal and don't usually make someone's checklist of sins. These patterns of sin fall short of God's plan nonetheless and are sin whether they make our lists or not. Romans 14:23 reminds us, "Whatever is not from faith is sin." There are many other attitudes and values that are not from faith and do not make the usual sin check lists, but they are sinful just the same.

Sin in a biblical sense is much more than an external action; it is something that affects all of life. Sin means missing the mark, the mark being God's will for us. When we look at our lives we see that we miss the mark not just in external actions, but thoughts, attitudes, values, love...and I could go on and on. Sin does not come in a tidy package. Sin is a problem so large and extensive that only God can take care of it. When we realize the deep trouble that we are in, the sheer weight of our sin problem should crush us. But we have a savior. The realization of the magnitude of our sin and the corresponding grace of God spurs us on to treat others the way we were treated by God. Jesus said, "Do not judge. By what measure you measure with will be measured out to you." This verse does not mean we can't judge certain things as right or wrong. The verse tells us that we need to use the same standard of judgment that was used on us. The standard God uses, acknowledges that we have a huge sin problem that is more extensive than just external actions. The actions are a symptom of sinful motivations, assumptions, values, and thoughts. That same standard also states that it is not you or I who defeat the sin—it is God. Our sin problem is so deep and so large that we cannot deal with sin ourselves through a checklist or sin scoreboard watching. A small view of sin causes us to be like the Pharisees: judgmental, hypocritical, and wrong.

Sin (not just the little definition of sin) is to blame for our failure to hear God's voice. When we get stuck in sin God may let the natural outcome of the sin play itself out so that we will turn to Him. When sin brings us to a place where we are stuck, we are probably in a "time out." In "time out," God will speak to us in a way that draws us closer to Him and away from the sin. But let us not think that sin can fit in a tidy box and we have a formula for taking care of it. Sin is a much bigger problem and invades our motivations, thoughts, values, assumptions, and attitudes.

When we see the reality of our sin problem, and when we realize how God has dealt with sin, we judge ourselves and others differently. A proper view of sin changes how we address sin in our life. We confront sin by striving towards, and guiding others towards, the only one who can change us from the inside out—Jesus Christ who won the victory over sin and death.

Questions to Ponder

What is your concept of Satan? How does this conception influence your life, if at all?

After reading this section, do you consider your concept of Satan and sin helpful or hurtful in relating to God?

How does the broader concept of sin change the way you think about yourself, about God, and about others?

Looking in the Mirror
—A Time to Reflect

Why do you do what you do? There are many reasons why we feel compelled to always be doing something: the esteem rush, the adrenaline rush, our culture, the hype, social proof, our disposition, our church. The common thread behind all these reasons is that they are all the wrong motivations for action. These motivations, even if subconscious, distract us from actually doing things for the right reason—hearing the voice of God. When all our actions are an outflow of our connection to God, then we do everything in His power and all that we do is a part of His plan. This is a Jesus type of life where "all that we see our Father doing, we do."

In contrast, when we do things from compulsion we usually hurt other people, our relationship with God, and ourselves. We also end up being more ineffective in the very task we set out to do. Because God loves us, He will give us a "time out" so we can hear His voice and live the right way and with the right motives.

God dealt with Moses in just such a way. When Moses was still a young man he saw the hard labor of his fellow Israelites. Someone needed to do something about it! Moses decided he was that someone. We don't know why Moses chose to do what he did. The Bible does not tell us if it was for esteem, an adrenaline rush, or his disposition. We do know that his actions were not a result of hearing the voice of God. Here is what happened:

> Now it came about in those days, when Moses had grown up, that he went out to his brethren and looked on their hard labors; and he saw an Egyptian beating a Hebrew, one of his brethren. So he looked this way and that, and when he saw there was no one around, he struck down the Egyptian and hid him in the sand. He went out the next day, and behold, two Hebrews were fighting with each other; and he said to the offender, "Why are you striking your companion?" But he said, "Who made you a prince or a judge over us? Are you intending to kill me as you killed the Egyptian?" Then Moses was afraid and said, "Surely the matter has become known." When Pharaoh heard of this matter, he tried to kill Moses. But Moses fled from the presence of Pharaoh and settled in the land of Midian. (Exodus 2: 11-15)

Moses tried to become a leader of Israel and deliver at least one Israelite from the hand of the Egyptian oppressors. Was delivering Israelites a good thing? Yes, but Moses' actions were not a result of hearing the voice of God. Moses' actions failed miserably and he nearly got himself killed. He needed to learn how to hear the voice of God and act in response to an encounter with God. To accomplish this change in Moses, God gave Moses a "time out."

Moses could no longer do what he had planned or what was familiar. Moses was in the land of Midian for approximately a half a century before he would ever go back to Egypt. Moses was in "time out."

You know the rest of the story; Moses did hear the voice of God, and in response to God's voice, Moses went down to Egypt. Moses performed many incredible feats in Egypt, but all his actions were a result of hearing the voice of the great I AM. By the end of the Exodus, Moses accomplished all that he had tried to do when he was young and much more. The difference was that after his "time out," Moses acted because he heard God's voice and not because of compulsion.

Moses was able to accomplish many incredible deeds once he learned to listen to God. Great accomplishments, however, are not the best part of listening to God. The best part is that we receive the most valuable possession in the universe—a closer relationship with the eternal, transcendent Father.

After God gave Moses a "time out," Moses *lived* in response to God's voice. Because of this connection to God, Moses lived a life of impact and a life in relationship to God. By the end of Moses' life, Exodus 33: 11 tells us, "Thus the LORD used to speak to Moses face to face, just as a man speaks to his friend." Will you be able to say that by the end of your life? Will you take a "time out" to hear God's voice and cultivate a life of responding to Him? If you begin to respond to God's voice instead of a compulsion then, like Moses, you will do great things and God will begin to speak to you "as a man speaks to his friend."

If you are like me, you read a book like this one, or hear a sermon you agree with, and you want to go do something about it. May I suggest sitting back for a few days and discussing with God and a loved one what you may have learned about yourself and what you need to better understand. This should not be an exercise in navel gazing or self-analysis paralysis. Rather, you should be looking over the course of your life and seeing where God's hand has been in your life. Can you identify any times where God may have given you a "time out"? Perhaps now you look at those times differently. You may remember past ministries or task in a different light as you ask yourself, "Why do I choose to do the things I do?" The goal of this reflection is to re-hear what God may have been saying to you in "time outs" past. It is also helpful to recognize the things that especially distract you from hearing God's voice. If you know that you feel compelled to perform for an esteem rush, then you listen to God even more carefully in esteem giving tasks. For example, if my wife is talking to me while I am reading, I know that I can't hear her. If, however, I am working on the car, I can listen fine. Reading distracts me, fixing stuff doesn't. Knowing my weaknesses changes how I approach the tasks and how I listen. If I am fixing something I don't have to drop everything to listen to my wife. If I hear my wife's voice while I am reading, however, I know I need to stop if I want to receive her message. What are the activities or tasks in your life that you must stop doing from time to time to receive your

Heavenly Father's message?

It is said that those who don't learn from history are doomed to repeat it. You have a history, a history of hearing or not hearing God's voice. You have a history of performing many tasks for many different reasons. Will you take a "time out" now and listen to what God has to say about your life, about why you do what you do, and about the health of your relationship with Him? Will you begin this process so that many years from now, like Moses, it will be said that, "The LORD speaks to him face to face, just as a man speaks to his friend."

Questions to Ponder

We have looked at many reasons for why we choose to do what we do. Of the reasons addressed so far, which would you say have the most influence in your life: the esteem rush, the adrenaline rush, our culture, the hype, social proof, your disposition, your church?

As you look over the course of your life, can you identify any points when God may have given you a "time out"? Do you look at these times differently now?

Stop! Take some time to look over the questions and key concepts from previous chapters. Do some praying and thinking about your personal history with God and why you choose to do what you do. Write down key areas or words that you feel the Lord is laying on your heart.

Part 5
When God No Longer Needs to Give a "Time Out"

Introduction to the Solution

By now you may be thinking, "I am a 'do' junkie. I demonize people who get in the way of my fix. I live in a country that promotes my addiction. I go to a church that encourages my habit. The only thing I do right is sleep." The bad news is that you can't enter cryogenic hibernation (a. la. Ted Williams and Walt Disney) while you are still alive. Besides, sleeping all the time, no matter how well you do it, really doesn't fix the problem. The good news is that you already have the solution. If you have a relationship with Christ, even if it is dysfunctional, then you already have what you need to get on the path of doing things for, and because of, relationship.

Many couples will testify that their relationship started off bad, but grew in intimacy and maturity eventually. So it is with you and God. You may be so busy that you rarely hear God's voice. You may be so accustomed to doing spiritual tasks for esteem that you have trouble discerning what is from God and what is from your need to keep up your image. You may be wondering why God doesn't give you more "time outs" since you rarely do anything as an outflow of relationship. Despite all these shortcomings, if you have placed your faith in Christ, you *still* have a relationship with God. The apostle Paul states it this way;

"But in all these things we overwhelmingly conquer through Him who loved us. For I am convinced that neither death, nor life, nor angels, nor principalities, nor things present, nor things to come, nor powers, nor height, nor depth, nor any other created thing, will be able to separate us from the love of God, which is in Christ Jesus our Lord." (Romans 8:37-39)

We may be junkies, but we are God's junkies. As our Father, God will not abandon us. He will keep working to free us so that we can be in intimate relation with Him. A little earlier in Romans 8 (verse 32) Paul states, "He who did not spare His own Son, but delivered Him over for us all, how will He not also with Him freely give us all things?" God is so passionate for us that He even sent His own son to restore this broken relationship. If God went to such lengths to establish this relationship before we were even born, how much more will he continue to work in us to free us from that which hinders our relationship now? Giving us a "time out" is one way that God will illuminate and remove the things that distract us from Him. A parent gives a child a "time out" not to separate the child from their love, but to separate the child from the distractions. Indeed, the "time out" is because of love. Likewise, if you have placed your faith in Jesus then know that nothing can separate you from the love of God.

While we have the solution to our deafness to God and compulsion to do already, the problem is living so that our connection becomes a visible reality in our everyday lives. Our need to do impairs our relationship, but relationship with God is the answer to breaking our compulsion to do. Our need to do is a habit. For example, people overeat because eating makes them feel good. They gain weight and don't feel good about themselves, so they eat more because it makes them feel good, which makes them gain more weight...this cycle is similar for those who have a "do" habit. We compulsively do and our busyness prevents us from hearing God. We know we aren't living the way God wants so we work harder to compensate. We complete many tasks, but we do not have the intimate, powerful relationship that God created us for. We sense that we aren't living for real and we are driven even more—but it is in the relationship that we would find a solution. No, this isn't a catch 22. Like all bad habits, the cyclical habit to do can be broken.

God, in His love, has given me "time outs" to break my habit to do. God can and will give you a "timeout" as well. May I suggest that you be proactive about the process and don't wait for the discomfort of a "time out." However, don't try to break your habit with the mindset that this is a steel cage battle to the death between you and the habit. You will probably lose. As said above, God is in the middle of this process and you must have the mindset that God will be doing the majority of the work inside you. That is what faith is: the trust that the God who saved you from the fires of hell is also interested in saving your life here on earth. Faith is trusting God with your whole life in all situations, not trusting in your own abilities. When you start looking to God to straighten out your motivations and break you out of the "do" habit you are on the right track. When you go to God, your relationship grows, and when your relationship is growing God doesn't need to give you a "time out" (as much).

Questions to Ponder

Have you trusted Christ and His work on the cross to restore you to a loving relationship with God? Or does this whole "relationship" thing seem like hollow Christian jargon?

If, through faith in Christ, you know that you will spend eternity with God, do you also trust that God wants a relationship with you now?

Meditate on Romans 8:32, "He who did not spare His own Son, but delivered Him over for us all, how will He not also with Him freely give us all things?"

Do you feel that God is that passionate for your heart? How does the crucifixion demonstrate God's love? (See Romans 5:8) Does the crucifixion of Christ help you to trust God more?

The Biblical Principle for Breaking Bad Compulsions

Let's assume you trust God to break your habit to do. You don't know, however, how that trust should play out in your everyday life. What is your part in this? Well, in the following chapters there are some suggestions as to how you can give yourself a "time out," to hear the voice of God. Incorporating some of these suggestions into your life is a way of breaking the habit to do as you become more intentional about stopping and listening to God. However, there is an overarching principle to breaking any sin habit or compulsion. All of our attempts at intentionally giving ourselves a "time out" must flow from this principle. This principle is articulated in Romans 7 and 8. Because these scriptures are the key to understanding how we are to participate in God's work of freeing us from sin habits, I have devoted this chapter to going through this passage of scripture.

Romans 7 and 8 are the Apostle Paul's answer for breaking any sin habit, which includes our habit to do. Some of the verses in Chapter 8 have been alluded to earlier, but let us take a deeper look into these chapters to learn God's plan for breaking sin patterns in our life. We pick up Paul's argument at Romans 7:4.

"Therefore, my brethren, you also were made to die to the Law through the body of Christ, so that you might be joined to another, to Him who was raised from the dead, in order that we might bear fruit for God. For while we were in the flesh, the sinful passions, which were aroused by the Law, were at work in the members of our body to bear fruit for death. But now we have been released from the Law, having died to that by which we were bound, so that we serve in newness of the Spirit and not in oldness of the letter."

The "therefore" in Paul's argument refers back to the fact that believers have died to the law and are no longer bound to the Old Testament law but bound to Christ. Being joined to Christ is the key to breaking free from our sin habit. The law, however, is an inadequate way of breaking a sin habit. Remember, this sin habit can be our addiction to do, or a sin habit concerning lustful thoughts, or any other pattern of sin in our life. Paul is putting forth a principle that can be applied to any situation where we try to overcome sin. It is clear that the "law" isn't effective in overcoming sin. Although Paul is referring to the Old Testament law specifically, this principle applies to any law we try to live by. This even includes laws like; "I need to be more loving." or "Don't lust" or "Be more patient." The law is any command or precept that instructs us what to do or not do. Paul argues that the law actually arouses the sinful passions that we are trying to overcome. I am sure his readers thought, "Hey Paul, God gave the Old Testament law, are you saying the law is bad?"

Anticipating the question, Paul continues:
"What shall we say then? Is the Law sin? May it never be! On the contrary, I would not have come to know sin except through the Law; for I would not have known about coveting if the Law had not said, 'You shall not covet.' But sin, taking opportunity through the commandment, produced in me coveting of every kind; for apart from the Law sin is dead. I was once alive apart from the Law; but when the commandment came, sin became alive and I died; and this commandment, which was to result in life, proved to result in death for me; for sin, taking an opportunity through the commandment, deceived me and through it killed me. So then, the Law is holy, and the commandment is holy and righteous and good."
Why is the law an inadequate way of breaking a sin habit? It is inadequate because it merely informs us what is unlawful. As Paul stated it, if he hadn't heard the law, "You shall not covet" he wouldn't have known that coveting was wrong. Coveting is wrong because it goes against God's nature and God informs us through the commandments that He doesn't like coveting. So the law, or commandment, is good because it is from God. Other commandments such as love the Lord your God, and love your neighbor, are also good. Hopefully, as you read this book you also realized that your compulsive doing can interfere with your relationship with God and you need to make changes in order to follow the command, "Let us press on to know the LORD." (Hosea 6:3)
The problem with any command (O.T. law or otherwise) or biblical application is that they only inform

us what we should do or not do. Before we knew how we were to act—we really didn't think about it. We may or may not have followed the command, but it was an ignorant kind of sin and not a knowing rebellion against what we *know* God wants. And that is the rub, isn't it? Now that we do know, we still break the command. Now our action is no longer a sin alone, it is a sin coupled with open rebellion. That tendency prompted Paul to explain that the commandment, which was supposed to result in life, supposed to result in him being more in touch with God's will, resulted in his death. So does God give us the law (or any command) to be cruel and kill us? Paul continues:

"Therefore did that which is good become a cause of death for me? May it never be! Rather it was sin, in order that it might be shown to be sin by affecting my death through that which is good, so that through the commandment sin would become utterly sinful.

"For we know that the Law is spiritual, but I am of flesh, sold into bondage to sin. For what I am doing, I do not understand; for I am not practicing what I would like to do, but I am doing the very thing I hate. But if I do the very thing I do not want to do, I agree with the Law, confessing that the Law is good. So now, no longer am I the one doing it, but sin which dwells in me. For I know that nothing good dwells in me, that is, in my flesh; for the willing is present in me, but the doing of the good is not. For the good that I want, I do not do, but I practice the very evil that I do not want. But if I am doing the very thing I do not want, I am no longer the one doing it, but sin which dwells in me."

The apostle is now really addressing the heart of the problem when we try to break a sin habit through the system of the law. We hear and accept the command, whatever it is, and then we try to follow it. We want to follow the command, but the harder we try the more we seem to fail. We want to stop coveting, we want to stop esteem seeking, or we want to _____ (you fill in the blank) but we just can't. The fact that we want to follow the command means that we agree that the command is good. We have a sin habit that we want to kick, the knowledge that the behavior is a sin, the desire to act differently—but we just can't overcome it. We seem to have this sin in us that doesn't subject itself to our mind's commands. No matter how hard we try to follow a command or Biblical precept, this sin inside us doesn't listen. Paul further explains:

"I find then the principle that evil is present in me, the one who wants to do good. For I joyfully concur with the law of God in the inner man, but I see a different law in the members of my body, waging war against the law of my mind and making me a prisoner of the law of sin which is in my members. Wretched man that I am! Who will set me free from the body of this death? Thanks be to God through Jesus Christ our Lord! So then, on the one hand I myself with my mind am serving the law of God, but on the other, with my flesh the law of sin."

Paul likens the inner conflict of overcoming sin to a war. There is a battle between our mind, or inner man, and this "law of sin" in our body. Our inner man wants to serve the law of God. We want to break our compulsive doing that interferes with knowing God, or we want to stop being so judgmental, or we want to pray more, or etc. etc. etc. But whatever we want to do isn't achieved because our flesh serves the law of sin, which seeks the easiest path, the most self-centered path, the most rebellious path. In this war our house is divided and we lose almost every time.

Theologians often debate whether the apostle Paul is referring to his pre-Christian problems in dealing with sin or a problem that he is currently having as a Christian. I believe that he is mostly talking about his pre-Christian problem since he boldly proclaims that Christ has set him free from this cycle of death. However, I think that the pre—vs. post Christian issue doesn't really matter in understanding Paul's main point, which is whenever you try to use a system of law to break a sin habit, you will fail. Christians who are no longer under the law can still act as if they are under the law when trying to break a sin habit. Instead of joining ourselves to Christ, who set us free from the law (7:4) and sin—we just try harder. We try and use our will to follow God and beat down our will to sin. What we do with our sin habits can be likened to a steel cage match. If you have ever watched "professional" wrestling (the kind with Hulk Hogan, Andre the Giant, and Stone Cold Steve Austin) you have probably seen a steel cage match. A big steel cage is put over the ring so that no one can escape. This is a fight to the end. There is no running away from the ring. Whoever is lying unconscious and bloody in the middle of the ring is the loser. Whoever is left standing and in control is the winner. Unfortunately when we go into the steel cage with a sin habit, our obedience to the command is usually left paralyzed, but that old sin habit is still standing and in control. Then we really understand what Paul meant when he said that trying to follow the command is a good idea, but it kills us every time.

Whenever we try to use our willpower to follow a command or biblical precept, we are living as if we are "under the law." Although the law is good, it does not justify us before God because we don't keep the law even when we become like a slave and use everything in our flesh to follow the law. The law is good, but we fall short in trying to make it a reality in our life. This is the shortcoming of the law. The writer of Hebrews agrees, saying, "For if that first covenant had been faultless, there would have been no occasion sought for a second." The fault wasn't in the law, or first covenant, but in the following of the law. This inability to follow the law made us guiltier, since rebellion against the commandment of God was added to the sin. This cycle of condemnation is at work whenever we put ourselves under a law, whether we are Christians or not. Paul's point is that Christians don't have to subject themselves to this "body of death." Christ has set us free from the law.

In Chapter 8, Paul moves from what *not* to do in dealing with a sin habit to what one needs to do. He writes:

" Therefore there is now no condemnation for those who are in Christ Jesus. For the law of the Spirit of life in Christ Jesus has set you free from the law of sin and of death. For what the Law could not do, weak as it was through the flesh, God did: sending His own Son in the likeness of sinful flesh and as an offering for sin, He condemned sin in the flesh, so that the requirement of the Law might be fulfilled in us, who do not walk according to the flesh but according to the Spirit. For those who are according to the flesh set their minds on the things of the flesh, but those who are according to the Spirit, the things of the Spirit. For the mind set on the flesh is death, but the mind set on the Spirit is life and peace, because the mind set on the flesh is hostile toward God; for it does not subject itself to the law of God, for it is not even able to do so, and those who are in the flesh cannot please God."

We first must realize that Jesus is the one who justified us. The law could not justify us "weak as it was through the flesh." As was said, the law simply revealed that we were sinners *and* rebellious. But what the law couldn't do, Jesus did. Jesus, as an "offering for sin" satisfied the debt that we owed as sinners against God. We are now without sin in God's eyes and there is no condemnation for us. We are no longer bound to the law because the law has been met, or fulfilled, already by Jesus on our behalf. Our gut reaction, our primary assumption must be that Jesus made us right. No matter how much we follow or don't follow a biblical precept or command is a secondary consideration. Christ has set us free. *End of story.* I know you are thinking, "Yea, I know this already." But do you? If Christ alone has freed us then when we are presented with a biblical command, why is our first reaction to assess our actions? If we are not keeping the command, we make a plan to be better. If we are following the command, we are proud. Our gut reaction isn't "Oh thank you Jesus—I am right already because of you." We must be truly Christ centered. We are bound to *Him* now, not to a command, not to a religion, not to a moral code, not to a set of religious acts. Our justification is centered on Christ. Our deep, gut conviction must be that we have already been made right by Christ alone. If this truth is not the lifeblood of our soul then our living righteously is already compromised.

The same Christ who justified us eternally in the sight of God will enable us to live our life righteously in this life (sanctification). The key is the same. Our sanctification, like our justification, is centered on Christ. Sanctification is the process in which we become more set apart to God and more like Christ. Sanctification includes breaking sin habits or anything that hinders us from being Christ-like (i.e. compulsive doing or esteem seeking). If we try to sanctify ourselves, by trying harder to follow a command, we are walking according to the flesh. The mind set on anything other than Christ leads to failure and an inability to achieve the very thing we desire (As Paul pointed out above, "because the mind set on the flesh is hostile toward God; for it does not subject itself to the law of God, for it is not even able to do so"). No matter how hard we try, or our motivation for trying, if we are following a command by using our flesh, as the above scripture states, "we cannot please God." We cannot please God because not only do we fail at following the command, we try to complete in our flesh what God initiated through His Spirit. As Paul wrote in Galatians, "Are you so foolish? Having begun by the Spirit, are you now being perfected by the flesh?" Our deliverance and our victory over any sin habit are found in Christ. Our mind must be set on the Spirit—it must be God centered. When we focus on the command, on trying harder, on judging our performance, we lose touch with our solution. We lose touch with Christ. We go back to walking in the flesh. Paul continues:

"However, you are not in the flesh but in the Spirit, if indeed the Spirit of God dwells in you. But if anyone does not have the Spirit of Christ, he does not belong to Him. If Christ is in you, though the body is dead because of sin, yet the spirit is alive because of righteousness. But if the Spirit of Him who raised Jesus from the dead dwells in you, He who raised Christ Jesus from the dead will also give life to your mortal bodies through His Spirit who dwells in you."

If Jesus has truly justified us then God in the person of the Holy Spirit dwells in us. This is the same Holy Spirit who raised Jesus from the dead. That power that gave life to Jesus will give life to us. We are no longer subject to this "body of death," as Paul stated earlier. Instead, the righteousness of Christ is like a wellspring that feeds into our inner person and gives us life. We must stay attached to this life source by setting our minds on Christ and the fact that He makes us right eternally. We also stay attached by setting our minds on the Spirit and His power to live righteously through us now. Our living is more like riding, riding on the Holy Spirit who will cause us to live differently from the inside out. Once we set our minds on the flesh, we are done for. That is what Paul goes on to say in this last section:

"So then, brethren, we are under obligation, not to the flesh, to live according to the flesh—for if you are living according to the flesh, you must die; but if by the Spirit you are putting to death the deeds of the body, you will live. For all who are being led by the Spirit of God, these are sons of God. For you have not received a spirit of slavery leading to fear again, but you have received a spirit of adoption as sons by which we cry out, 'Abba! Father!' The Spirit Himself testifies with our spirit that we are children of God, and if children, heirs also, heirs of God and fellow heirs with Christ, if indeed we suffer with Him so that we may also be glorified with Him."

Trying harder didn't save us, so we are no longer under any obligation to that method. We are only under obligation to God and it is through our focus on Him that we can follow those commands. We are riding on the coattails of His Spirit, as God lives through us. Naturally, the Spirit lives righteously and as long as we are clinging to Him we live wherever He is. This is not a spirit of slavery or fear that we are not measuring up to some law. This is the Holy Spirit who reassures us that we are God's beloved children and that we already have all that we need to become like Him. We no longer have only *our* spirit versus our flesh. We now also have the Holy Spirit of God and all His power, guidance, and gifts. We don't have an external set of laws to strive for, we now have an internal advocate who seeks to sanctify us from the inside out. He is our answer when we are stuck in a sin habit. When we want to stop being compulsive about doing things because we want to hear God's voice, our relationship with Jesus, and the presence of the Holy Spirit, is the answer. Our mind must be set on Christ and our dependence must be on Christ for justification and sanctification.

This section of Romans must be our guide when addressing any sinful behavior in our life. It is clear that the guiding principle is to depend on and focus on Christ alone to set us free. While our natural inclination may be to try harder, our hope lies not in struggling to obtain what we don't have, but resting in what we have already. We have Immanuel—"God with us." Nothing can separate us from God and His love. We are irrevocably adopted as His children. This relationship holds the keys to our abundant life both here and in Heaven. Doers have a difficult time swallowing this pill. We want a method, a checklist, an action plan. These techniques are not God's solution. God gives us a "time out" so that we hear HIS voice. God gives us a "time out" so that we will build a relationship with Him—not build a plan or method. If we look to some method or action plan to save us from our deeply ingrained sinfulness then we are trying to use the sin of self-sufficiency to defeat our sinful compulsions.

In the following chapters I will share some ideas that may help you focus on God. As the above scripture shows, it is our focus on God that will free us from any sin habit, including compulsive doing. Reading this book, the ideas for giving yourself a "time out"—none of these are the answer. They are all means to an end, suggestions to help you focus on God. After all, God gives you a "time out" in order to hear HIS voice, not mine.

If you choose to follow some of the ideas I present in subsequent chapters, know that they must flow from your conviction that focusing on Christ is the answer. The second part of the overall principle found in Romans 7 & 8 is that we are dependant on Christ alone to free us. This conviction must descend from our heads to our hearts. There is no easy way to do this. This principle must soak into your soul. Ironically, as you mistakenly depend on your will to sanctify yourself and then fail, this principle will sink deeper into your soul. Whole, deep, dependent living is a process. For now you may need to simply acknowledge this fact. Confess to God that you agree that you are helpless to sanctify yourself. Ask Him to let this truth take root in your heart. As you live your life in God's presence, being dependant (and slipping up and being not so dependant) this truth will take root. Focus and dependence on God is a life long process grounded in Christ's loving sacrifice on the cross.

When it comes to life on this earth, we are trying to put ourselves in the presence of God enough that His grace transforms us[9]. It is like getting a suntan. If we want a tan we need to be in the sun. We don't really do the tanning, the sun does. Our part is getting out of the house. Our "doing" keeps us in the house. All of our sin habits keep us in the shadows of a darkened house.

The next section contains suggestions to help us get out of the house. These are not the solution to our habit to do—God is. Of course, we can take these suggestions and practice them compulsively. If, however, our goal is to be in close relationship to God then these are means that may help achieve that end. But we must keep in mind the over arching principle that the solution is a focus, and dependence, on Christ. All these suggestions can be considered ways of giving yourself a "time out" so that you can set your mind on God. Like a Father with a child, God wants us to be able to mature to the point that we self regulate. Maturity means that God may give us "time outs" (Amen to that) when we are young. But His hope is that one day He no longer needs to give us "time outs" because when we start to become spiritually deaf to Him, we give ourselves a kind of "time out" so that we can refocus on His voice.

Questions to Ponder

What "Law" have you been trying to follow?

Why is the law an inadequate way of breaking a sin habit?

Can you think of a recent example in your life when you would echo Paul's words, "For what I am doing, I do not understand; for I am not practicing what I would like to do, but I am doing the very thing I hate?"

What is your normal strategy for following a biblical precept? Can you relate to the "steel cage?"

When confronted with a biblical command is your deep, gut conviction that you have already been made right by Christ alone?

Where is your default focus when confronted with your own spiritual shortcomings?

Were you disappointed when the answer to breaking bad compulsions turned out to be, "Focus and dependence on God in a life long process grounded in Christ's loving sacrifice on the cross." and not a checklist or method?

The Sabbath—An Intentional "Time Out" for God

After God finished creating this universe, He took a break. God doesn't get tired, so why did He take a rest? I believe He took a rest because for a time, there was no need to do anything else. After creation, it was time for God to relate to and enjoy what He had made. I also believe that God was providing a powerful example. If God, who needs no break, took a break—then people, who tire easily, should take a break. Whatever the reason God rested, scripture tells us that God wants us to take a "time out." Look through all the Sabbath scriptures in the Bible and it becomes clear that God wants us to have "time outs," or Sabbaths to ensure that we have time to connect with God. In the Hebrew world, one could become caught up with work because it was a struggle just to survive. The compulsion to constantly do things arose from a need for security rather than a need for esteem or a chemical rush. If one was constantly working, then one felt more secure from starvation or invasion. Although this reason may seem nobler than our modern day reasons for being addicted to busyness, God knew that it was equally distracting. Whenever people are driven to constantly do things the end result is always difficulty in hearing the voice of God. God wanted Israel to have at least one day out of seven to work on knowing Him. Exodus 31:12-17 explains it this way:

> "The LORD spoke to Moses, saying, 'But as for you, speak to the sons of Israel,' saying, 'You shall surely observe My Sabbaths; for this is a sign between Me and you throughout your generations, *that you may know that I am the LORD who sanctifies you*. Therefore you are to observe the Sabbath, for it is holy to you. Everyone who profanes it shall surely be put to death; for whoever does any work on it, that person shall be cut off from among his people. For six days work may be done, but on the seventh day there is a Sabbath of complete rest, *holy to the LORD*; whoever does any work on the Sabbath day shall surely be put to death. So the sons of Israel shall observe the Sabbath, to *celebrate the Sabbath throughout their generations as a perpetual covenant. It is a sign* between Me and the sons of Israel forever; for in six days the LORD made Heaven and earth, but on the seventh day He ceased from labor, and was refreshed." (Italics mine)

This 'time out" in the week was for Israel to know that God sanctifies them. This is the overarching principle that we spoke of earlier. We are dependant on God to sanctify us and grow us into what we were meant to be. We cannot sanctify ourselves. Taking a "time out" is a step of faith as we acknowledge that we can rest because whatever we are working for (righteousness, security, material things, happiness) is dependant on God—not us.

In the above scripture, the Sabbath harkens back to creation. The Sabbath was considered a sign and a covenant as God's people remembered that God is the creator of all that they saw and knew. As Israel mimicked weekly what God did in the beginning, they were acknowledging that God is the creator. In this way the Sabbath was a "sign" that pointed them to God. The Sabbath was a covenant in that God set apart (sanctified) Israel as His own people and Israel in turn set a day apart to celebrate and connect with the God that had established this special relationship.

For Christians, the principle of rest remains. God rested, so we need to rest unto the Lord. God sets us apart to be in relationship with Him so we set time apart towards this relationship. We carve out a day of rest that facilitates our connection with God. It is not that the remaining part of our week is not God's, we still work in His name, play in His name, doing everything unto Him. However, we need to give our bodies at least one day of rest to *quietly or restfully* remember God's creative work and His re-creative work in saving us from death and buying us with His blood. God's work allows us to enjoy God all day, everyday, directly through His Son and by the Holy Spirit.

The Sabbath principle is a gift. For the Israelites it was a commandment that required at least one day of rest to remember God, go to temple, etc. The command was an effective external control to give the Israelites merciful rest and a time when they could do nothing other than worship God.

In the new covenant the Sabbath principle is still a gift. We no longer need external controls to bring us to God. The Holy Spirit living within us drives us to live every day for God. The Holy Spirit sanctifies our work, play, and everything we do. While every day is God's, we still need rest from doing tasks in order to focus on God. We need time to refocus so that our work or play will draw us closer to God instead of distract us from hearing Him. The Sabbath principle may require rest even from the work of the ministry. Even ministry can distract and hinder us from hearing God if our focus is on the *tasks* of ministry.

As God's children, we crawl into the lap of our Father and spend time with Him. Not just once a week for a day, but every day we spend a little rest time with the Father. It is important to not think of the Sabbath principle as only a one-day-a-week practice. The principle extends to our daily lives as we strive to carve out a mini "time out" every day: A time when we can be still and know that He is God (Psalm 46:10), a time when we can be silent and listen for His voice.

Is there a day, or a good chunk of a day, that you can spend resting in the presence of God? Perhaps Sunday is a good day for you. For me, Sunday is often a busy day spent doing church work. I previously set aside Mondays as my Sabbath, but I am currently taking a chunk of Friday and a then a few hours on Wednesday. The goal is to have a sizeable time during the week when I can stop performing tasks and focus on the Father's voice. I have this same goal on a daily basis. For me, first thing in the morning is my best time to take a "time out" and connect with God. I know others who take a "time out" at night, or at lunch. The particular time doesn't matter, what matters is that I am intentional about building into my day a time to be still and know God. I have found that if I don't plan on this time, and specifically build it into my day, I don't follow through. Even when I actually set aside time in my day planner, I sometimes neglect this "time out." The important concept to remember is that taking a Sabbath is a means to an end. If a "time out" is missed, we are not ruined. We still have the end goal— relationship with God. We also still have the next minute, hour and day to connect with God. We build "time outs" in our schedule to hear God's voice, but hopefully they are just what we fall back on to make sure we have some connection time. The truth is, we can take mini "time outs" any time, anywhere. We use our planned "time outs" to hone our ability to hear the Father's voice all day. It requires only a minute to kick back from the computer screen and check in with God. When we are stuck in traffic we can tell the Father we are ready to listen. When the kids are actually occupying themselves we can go to the next room and listen for His voice. What begins with our planned Sabbaths, with God's grace, can become a whole life tuned to hearing the Father's voice. This is the kind of life that the monks of old strived for and a life that even us Joe Shmoes can taste.

Questions to Ponder

Do you currently follow the Sabbath principle?

What day, or parts of days would be easiest for you to set aside? Could your spouse or friend hold you accountable and help you keep a Sabbath time?

When is the best time for you to take a "mini time out" each day?

Becoming a Monk

Have you ever wanted to get a nice bald patch on the top of your head and wear a long camel hair robe? No, me either, but I do want to be a monk. There were (and are) some monks that totally missed the boat. There were some monks trying to escape from family, some monks who liked the power that the medieval church gave them, and some monks who were monks out of superstition. There were (and are), however, some monks that were on to something spiritually. No, I don't mean the haircut, although I have seen some aging men reluctantly sporting the "tonsure" and I am on my way. What the monks were on to was their effort to include God in every aspect of their life. Every activity, no matter how mundane, was done in the presence of the Father. Monks sought to tune into the voice of God at any and all times. Listen to what William of St. Thierry, a monk of the 1100s, wrote in his work *The Golden Epistle*,

> "For that is your (a monk's) profession, to seek the very face of God which Jacob saw, he who said: 'I have seen the Lord face to face and yet my life was not forfeit.' To 'seek the face of God' is to seek

knowledge of him face to face, as Jacob saw him...this piety is the continual remembrance of God, an unceasing effort of the mind to know him, an unwearied concern of the affections to love him, so that, I will not say every day, but every hour finds the servant of God occupied in the labor of ascesis and the effort to make progress, or in the sweetness of experience and the joy of fruition. This is the piety concerning which the Apostle exhorts his beloved disciple in the words: 'Train yourself to grow up in piety; for training of the body avails but little, while piety is all-availing, since it promises well both for this life and for the next'. The habit (the robe) you wear promises not only the outward form of piety but its substance, in all things and before all things, and that is what your vocation demands."[10]

That is the kind of monk I want to be! William clearly stated that all the monk stuff, including the snazzy robe, is secondary to the monk's primary vocation of knowing God. The goal is "an unceasing effort of the mind to know him, an unwearied concern of the affections to love him." In short, the goal is relationship. To hone their relationship with God, and their ability to hear His voice, many monks went into an extended period of "time out." Their goal was the same one that has been written about in this book—remove the distractions, all the tasks, and focus on God's voice. In William's order, monks had what he called "cells" in which they spent their alone time with God. Of these "time outs" with God, William wrote:

"If anyone does not posses this (the desire to know God as written about above) in his heart, display it in his life, practice it in his cell, he is to be called not a solitary, but a man who is alone, and his cell is not a cell for him, but a prison in which he is immured. For truly to be alone is not to have God with one…the cell should never involve immurement imposed by necessity, but rather be the dwelling-place of peace, and inner chamber with closed door, a place not of concealment but of retreat."[11]

Twenty-first century Christians need a "cell," not a literal place as much as any place to go and connect with God. Like the monk's cell, "time outs" are not for us to be alone and hide ourselves from a stressful and hostile world. "Time outs" are "not for concealment, but retreat," retreat meaning openly resting in the company of the Father, Friend and Savior. The location is not important, but the monks saw the value of having a place where there were no distractions. Each monk had a place where there was nothing to do except connect with God in a transparent, honest, and meaningful way.

The goal of the "time out," or the cell, is to take time to hear God's voice and train ourselves. We train because at first we may only be able to hear God while solitary. The goal, however, is to eventually be able to listen to God when in a crowd or engaged in activity. This growth does not mean that one graduates from having to take "time outs." No matter how mature a Christian is he/she still needs time to focus on God alone. To use the theme of this book, it is like a child who needs a "time out" because there are too many distractions and they can't hear the parent's voice. When the child is almost an adult, they have hopefully matured to a point that when their parent speaks to them in the store they can immediately focus on the parent's voice. (However, when this child later gets married they may have to battle selective hearing when it comes to their spouse.) The parent-child relationship still needs some one-on-one time to continue growing—but doing things together actually helps the relationship rather than takes away from it. The goal of a monk is to live in God's presence and hear Him at *all* times, not just while alone or in "time out."

When the principle behind taking a "time out" (listening to God) begins to infiltrate all of life, then we are starting to "practice His presence" as Brother Lawrence describes it. Brother Lawrence was a 17th century monk who sought to knowingly enjoy God's presence in every aspect of his life. His life of devotion to hearing the Father's voice is described this way:

"That when he (Brother Lawrence) had thus in prayer filled his mind with great sentiments of that infinite Being, he went to his work appointed in the kitchen (for he was cook to the society); there having first considered severally the things his office required, and when and how each thing was to be done, he spent all the intervals of his time, as well before as after his work, in prayer.

That, when he began his business, he said to GOD, with a filial trust in Him, 'O my GOD, since Thou art with me, and I must now, in obedience to Thy commands, apply my mind to these outward things, I beseech Thee to grant me the grace to continue in Thy Presence; and to this end do Thou prosper me with Thy assistance, receive all my works, and possess all my affections.'

As he proceeded in his work, he continued his familiar conversation with his Maker, imploring His grace, and offering to Him all his actions.

When he had finished, he examined himself how he had discharged his duty; if he found well, he returned thanks to GOD; if otherwise, he asked pardon; and without being discouraged, he set his mind right again, and continued his exercise of the presence of GOD, as if he had never deviated from it. 'Thus,' said he, 'by rising after my falls, and by frequently renewed acts of faith and love, I am come to a state, wherein it would be as difficult for me not to think of GOD, as it was at first to accustom myself to it.'

As Bro. Lawrence had found such an advantage in walking in the presence of GOD, it was natural for him to recommend it earnestly to others; but his example was a stronger inducement than any arguments he could propose. His very countenance was edifying; such a sweet and calm devotion appearing in it, as could not but affect the beholders. And it was observed, that in the greatest hurry of business in the kitchen, he still preserved his recollection and Heavenly-mindedness. He was never hasty nor loitering, but did each thing in its season, with an even uninterrupted composure and tranquility of spirit. 'The time of business,' said he, 'does not with me differ from the time of prayer; and in the noise and clutter of my kitchen, while several persons are at the same time calling for different things, I possess GOD in as great tranquility as if I were upon my knees at the Blessed Sacrament.'"[12]

When I read about Brother Lawrence, I get that inner "YES!" "Yes," because I am happy that someone achieves such constant contact with God. "Yes," because I deeply desire to be in the Father's presence in this way.

Do you want to be a monk yet? I do. I want my primary profession to be knowing God and hearing His voice, like what William of St. Thierry wrote about. I want to be so deeply aware of God's presence that I can hear his voice even when I am doing dishes, like Brother Lawrence.

While monks would go off into their cells to hone their ability to hear God, they also had their faith community to spur them on once they were out of their cell. Younger monks had elders and all monks had one another to hold them to the task of knowing God. When a monk got too caught up in doing works for God, he hopefully had someone like Brother Lawrence step in to refocus him. The monks had a community to keep them focused and balanced.

Here in the 21st century, we non-monks also have a community to keep us focused. We have our church. Even if our church seems to be a distraction, there is nothing stopping us from carving out a group of like-minded believers that will hold us to our goal of being a monk. In a small group of believers we can help one another overcome things that distract us from God, and we can be co-laborers in striving to practice God's presence. Monks are experts in the art of giving themselves a "time out." Find others who desire to live in God's presence and spur one another on to becoming monks. (Robes and haircut optional)

Questions to Ponder

Are the goals of a monk, as talked about in this chapter, consistent with your goals?

Do you have a "cell" or place that facilitates your connection with God?

What are your feelings about the connection with God that Brother Lawrence had? Is this possible for you? Why or why not?

Re-hearing—"Time Out"
Prevention Through Journaling

The following is a common occurrence in the Greene household: I give one of my children a "time out" to ensure my instructions are heard clearly. I walk away confident that my child has understood me and listened to what I said. Ten minutes later I see the child doing the same thing that we had just talked about. I ask with frustration, "Why are you doing that again? Didn't I just explain why that is bad?" The response is, "I'm sorry, I forgot." What is amazing is that my child did actually forget. Yes, the heart to heart conversation occurred only ten minutes ago, but it doesn't take the child long to get caught up in doing stuff again. The child becomes so focused on doing that my instructions are quickly forgotten. Before we chuckle at the flightiness of youth, we should look in the mirror.

Every few months I look back through my journal and I usually find some word from God that I have since forgotten. I heard the message clearly and was impressed enough to write it down. As life started to kick into high gear, however, all the activity crowded the message from my active memory. The journal entry may have been prompted by a great "time out," but I either need another "time out" or I need to re-hear the message. Instead of being stuck in "time out," I prefer to re-hear the message. Journaling allows us to re-hear what God has said.

When I look through my journal and discover a forgotten encounter with God, I have two reactions. My first reaction is one of repentance for forgetting and not continuing in what God has said. My second reaction is thankfulness that I don't need another "time out" to hear the same message. As I read my journal, I can re-hear and reapply God's words. If I hadn't written anything down, the message would have remained forgotten.

The process of writing something down, in itself, helps us remember. Along with the mental image or impression from God, we have the visual and tactile impression from writing it down. In addition, we read that same encounter again in a month or in a year and if we still remember it, the message is reinforced. Journaling can be thought of as "time out" prevention. God gives us a message and through the process of journaling, the message is received and applied. God doesn't need to give us a "time out" because we have heard (or re-heard) what He has said to us.

The primary reason that I am writing this book is to re-hear the messages that God has impressed upon me in my "time outs." As I collect thoughts, memories, journal entries, and notes from my Bible, I start to see a pattern to God's hand in my life. The larger, deeper, and more eternal picture usually becomes clearer when we are able to look back over life and see what God has done.

Journaling, or writing, is the camera that captures the pictures of time spent with the Father. As these pictures are put together, an epic of personal salvation history and sanctification appear. Are there scenes missing from your life's epic story because you forgot them?

God often told the prophets to write down His words so that the people could re-hear His message after some time had passed. In Jeremiah 36: 2- 3, the Lord told Jeremiah the prophet:

"Take a scroll and write on it all the words which I have spoken to you concerning Israel and concerning Judah, and concerning all the nations, from the day I first spoke to you, from the days of Josiah, even to this day. Perhaps the house of Judah will hear all the calamity which I plan to bring on them, in order that every man will turn from his evil way; then I will forgive their iniquity and their sin."

God had spoken to the Israelites for some time and they didn't listen. God instructed Jeremiah to write the message down so the Israelites could re-hear "all the calamity which I plan to bring on them" and repent. In fact, when the King burned the scroll that Jeremiah had produced, God told Jeremiah to write the scroll again so that the message would be preserved and re-heard.

Ultimately, Israel did not heed the message and they were sent into the seventy-year "time out" known as the exile. The writings of Jeremiah would be a valuable teaching tool to the Israelites during and after the exile. Because the message was written down, the Israelites knew that God had indeed spoken as what was foretold came to pass. During the exile, Jeremiah's writings encouraged the Jewish people since God had also delivered a message that one day Israel would be restored. The people read and re-heard the message and it gave them hope. When their "time out" was over, the Jewish people preserved Jeremiah's writings so that generation after generation could re-hear the message that they had failed to hear.

The Bible is a collection of messages from God that we all need to hear and re-hear. God directed faithful men to preserve His words because He knew that every generation would need to re-hear some of the same teachings. In this sense, journaling does have biblical precedent. Of course, our journal writing is not on par with scripture, but it does serve to preserve the more particular, individual dealing between God and each one of us. God will not say or do something that contradicts His message in scripture. He does, however, deal with each of us particularly. When we start to doubt His individual dealings with us, when we forget God's words to us in particular, we have a choice. We can re-hear His words in our journals or we can wait for a "time out" to hear the message we did not hear the first (or twentieth) time. Of course, if we haven't journaled and have forgotten God's word to us then we don't have the opportunity to re-read (rehear) the message. We miss the blessing of being reminded that God is active and vocal in our lives here and now. Journaling preserves the epic history of God's personal dealings with each of us. This history can be brought to bear on our current faith struggles. We all need to be reminded and rehear all that God has said and done in our lives. Journaling preserves these personal, intimate dealings and reminds us that God is alive and active in our lives.

Questions to Ponder

How could you fit journaling into your life?

Can you remember a time when you forgot something that God impressed upon you, and needed to relearn it at a later time?

Invasion of the Prayer Snatchers

There is a wonderful spot not too far from my house in Massachusetts where there are two small waterfalls cascading around a large boulder. Built into the boulder is a natural granite chair where I like to sit and listen for God. This place is full of natural beauty, but I especially like the sound of the rushing water. When I first arrive at the waterfalls, or at any brook really, I am always surprised at how loud the water sounds. By the time I am ready to leave I am so accustomed to the sound of the water that I no longer hear it. At first, I hear the sound of the water whether I try to or not. Later, I have to focus my hearing to be able to hear the sound of the water.

I come to this place because this "disappearing water sound" is a reminder of how easily the voice of God gets tuned out in my life. For those of you who are not the outdoorsy type, just think about how loud your dishwasher sounds when you first turn it on. After a while, you go about the house and don't even realize when it stops running.

We stop hearing the falling water or the dishwasher partly because that is how the human brain works. Our brains (specifically, a part of our brains known as the reticular activating system) screen out background noise so we can focus on the task at hand. Screening out falling water and dishwashers can be handy, but screening out the ever-present God is always a tragedy. Because God can, and usually does, speak past our physical ears, our brains' reticular activating system is not really the problem. The real culprit is our short attention span and our spiritual attention deficit disorder. We have trouble staying focused on one thing for very long, even if it is something we need or enjoy, like the falling water or the voice of our Heavenly Father. Our attention shifts so easily.

Marketing firms have made a science out of catching people's attention. Research indicates that Americans are getting shorter attention spans, and marketers know this. Commercials are becoming more image-driven as so many companies strive to make an impression before the remote control goes "click." Americans and their children are being conditioned to take in an image or information quickly and move on. Not only are we consumers, we are now super-efficient consumers who take in as much as possible in as little time possible. It is no wonder that we have an attention deficit problem.

How this all plays out in terms of our relationship with God is obvious. In fact, I am sure you have felt the effects of our attention deficit culture during your prayer time. Does the following sound familiar: One day, you are actually disciplined enough to have an hour of "time out." You take a few minutes to open your Bible and ask God to speak to you through His word. You read a chapter of scripture and see a couple of interesting verses, after which you ask God to help your children, your spouse and your church. (Most people stop their "time out" here.) Feeling you want to really hear from God you leave your prayer line open and sit quietly, waiting for whatever God may say. About ten minutes later you realize that you haven't been open to God, you've been thinking about whatever task you need to begin after your "time out" is over. A little disappointed with yourself, you press on with the remaining thirty minutes and let God know that you are listening again.

Twenty minutes later the following thought fills your mind, "I wonder what happened to the credit card bill that I misplaced the other day. Can I get another one issued? Did I check under the pile of papers on the counter?" Once more you realize that you are not praying, listening, or connecting to God in any way. Frustrated that you were not praying or listening to God, you leave your "time out" early so you can at least get something done.

Oh yes, another "time out" ruined by an invasion of the prayer snatchers. Although the prayer snatchers have invaded Christian minds for centuries,[13] the American way of life leaves us particularly vulnerable to an invasion of these life-draining aliens. We want to listen to God and when we actually carve out some time to connect with Him, thoughts, alien to God and the purpose at hand, invade our heads and take our prayer time captive. Our devotional "time out" may have started well as God spoke to us through our Bible reading, but before God could elaborate and clarify what this word meant for our lives we are thinking about finding that lost credit card bill! With a short attention span, these prayer snatchers invade our mind and distract us from hearing God's voice.

How do we turn the invasion back? Prevention through a good defense is probably the best answer. Actively trying to cultivate a regular Sabbath time as written about in the previous chapter acclimatizes our minds to being open for an extended period of time. It is harder for the prayer snatcher to invade when our minds are in the habit of focusing on God. This habit doesn't develop if we give up on a "time out" because we were invaded the first several times we tried. No, habits take a while to develop and eventually the invasions become more infrequent. (However, these prayer snatchers are a tricky sort so we are always susceptible to a surprise attack).

Meditation is a helpful discipline to train our minds to have a longer attention span. I don't mean emptying your mind in an eastern religious sense, but readying your mind to receive what God may say to you. Meditation is intentionally focusing your mind to train your attention span. Meditating on a scripture, promise, or attribute of God to get your mind accustomed to extended focus may be helpful. Meditation may starts out as an "extended forced thinking" that feels unnatural. With time, however, you may develop a general ability to open your mind to God for an extended period of time. As with all habits, building up an acute and extended focus through practicing meditation takes time. This focus is also a means to an end. I know many non-believers who can focus their minds on the word "Ohm" for hours. They may have more attention span and more ability to focus than most people, but they do not have more of the God of our Lord Jesus Christ. Meditation in a Christian sense is building our minds' defenses against the thought invasions and building it towards extended focus on God.

Another preventive measure is using your short attention span and thirst for novelty to help instead of hinder. Go to a new or inspiring place for a "time out." For instance, after going three straight weeks to my waterfall I went to a scenic lookout. The overlook impressed me with the power and transcendence of God. Another time, I may go into my room and be impressed with the closeness and intimacy of God. I also like to read a chapter of a Christian book during my "time out" so that I can get a fresh perspective as God speaks through a fellow believer. By trying new places or things in our "time outs" we are attempting to walk up to the river anew so we can hear the water as we did at first. Of course, I don't mean new in a heretical sense, I mean new as in looking at the same diamond from a different angle. The market research gurus will tell you that attention spans are slightly longer for new things. We can focus on God longer, and prevent the invasion of the prayer snatchers, if we shake away from the same old routine. This change up may entail not journaling for a while because it has become ritual. We may need to fast to break free from our routine or pray with someone as part of our "time out." "The Spirit is willing but the flesh is weak" and that is why sometimes we need to trick our flesh. When we break free from our routine, it is harder for the prayer snatchers to invade and easier to keep our focus on God.

What is one to do in the middle of an invasion? Is there any way to turn back these pernicious thoughts once the invasion starts? A method that works for me (that I learned from Richard Foster)[14] is lifting up the invading thoughts to God. Here's how it works: You are praying or listening for God and you start thinking about that credit card bill. As soon as you realize that you are being invaded turn the invasion over to God. Pray about what you are thinking or feeling. Your prayer may sound something like this,

"God, I keep thinking about this bill. I know my finances are in your hand. Help me to find this bill and turn over the problem to you. Take this thought from my mind and hold it for now. Bring it back when I can deal with it effectively. As for now speak because your servant is listening."

You have engaged the invading thought, you have lifted it up to God, and now you are ready for whatever comes next. This method is effective for several reasons. Because you have actually engaged the thought, it doesn't just keep banging on the door in the background of your mind. However, aliens in your house are very distracting if they stay; so you ask for God's help in dealing with the problem. Not only does lifting the thought up to God keep your focus on God, but it actually asks God to bring His power to bear on the problem. Lastly, this method doesn't throw the baby out with the bath water. Perhaps God is the one bringing this thought into your head. He often speaks to me in this manner. If you give an invading thought to God to hold and He keeps returning it to you, perhaps He is speaking to you. If you continue to be invaded by credit card thoughts, then meditate on that thought. Ask God what about the bill is really getting you worried. Is the bill itself the issue or finances as a whole? Perhaps God is using the invading thought as a goad to speak to you about the larger issue. Perhaps He wants to guide you in that area. By lifting up the invading prayer snatcher to God, you can discern if the thought is a distraction or if it comes in peace (or from the Prince of Peace, to be exact).

What frustrates us all is when we actually show discipline in our life and carve out a Sabbath time, or monkishly practice God's presence, or journal, and that "time out" gets invaded and wasted on thoughts alien to our God connection. We are not helpless, however. We can build up our defenses to prevent the invasion of our "time outs" and we can call in God's heavy artillery. Whatever method we decide to employ is a means to an end—an end where we will enjoy a time of hearing God's still small voice. Instead of invasion, we will enjoy a time when God's voice is just as clear and soothing as when we first walked up to that cascade of living water.

Questions to Ponder

How often do the prayer snatchers invade your quite time?

Can you identify certain situations that invite invasion?

How do you think you could best train your mind to prevent invasion and stay open to God?

Wait Watchers

Americans find it very difficult to wait. Our inability to wait is linked to our short attention span and why thoughts invade our prayer time. Waiting and listening to God for an hour is difficult for many people. Waiting on God to speak during our prayer time is just a part, however, of a greater need to wait on God to work in all circumstances of life. Waiting of any kind has come under attack in modern civilization. We have a drive-thru culture. We like things fast and made to order. If something takes too long, we abandon it since few things are worth the wait. The time it takes to wait can be used elsewhere.

Americans incorrectly consider waiting a waste of time instead of a time for growth. If we want growth, we must wait. Growing is not something we can "get done." As a compulsive doer I would often try to make myself grow. I would try to grow myself by reading Christian growth books, finishing off my devotions, or working at ministry. The problem is that growth is a process and not a task. If true growth is to happen, we must wait and allow time to pass. We can plant a tree and water it, fertilize it, prune it, and weed around it. Despite all this activity, we still must wait for growth and we can't force growth by doing more things. Growth happens when we are close to the source of our growth—Jesus. The essence of waiting on God is not being satisfied with accomplishments or tasks, but only being satisfied with closeness to God. We are waiting on *God*, not for something to get accomplished.

When we wait on God, we don't just twiddle our thumbs. Waiting on God is an active obedience, not a passive time of stagnation. God accomplishes much through us, but it is the *Holy Spirit* who is at work in us and through us to accomplish His will. A large part of growing in our relationship with God, and our ability to hear His voice, is waiting on God to accomplish things. As a compulsive doer, this drives me crazy! Not only do I want the task to be done, I want to be the one doing it. After all, there are goals that I want to accomplish and they won't get done unless I take charge. Or will they?

One of the precepts of this book is that we must not "do" out of compulsion, but from an encounter with God. We hear God's voice and then we follow that lead. Our list of things to do (or goals) should be God's goals for us. If our "to do" list and goals coincide with God's, then we know that He will make sure the tasks are accomplished. Our tendency is to get a sense of what God wants and immediately go charging out. When we charge out we leave God behind. It is like a soldier who hears his orders and then goes charging to the front line alone, without support, without covering fire. This soldier may be in the right place, but he is there at the wrong time and without the real firepower (i.e. God). If God has chosen a strategic task for you, then He will see that task through. He will not, however, throw away the ultimate, strategic war plan to accomplish a tactical victory. God's ultimate war plan is to secure the trust and love of your soul in relationship to Him. This plan means that God will accomplish stunning victories through your life, but only as you wait on Him. The waiting is not passive but active as you learn to trust the general's judgment and carry out his orders. Our active waiting on God is more like training than standing in line.

A wise general will not send untrained men into battle. The general will take the necessary time to train his soldiers so that they grow into a cohesive fighting unit. As we wait for the task, or battle, we actively come to understand the ways of the commander and trust him with our lives. Through discipline and training we acquire the tools to accomplish lofty goals. No matter how ready we think we are, we still must wait on the general to say, "Go." He will say "Go" when he knows we are ready, when the circumstances are ripe, and when he has his firepower concentrated on an area. Until that time we wait on the general and watch for the sign to proceed.

King David was a military man who understood how to take and give orders. David was primarily, though, a man after God's own heart. Through Samuel, God anointed David the king of Israel despite the fact that Saul was still king at the time. Fourteen years passed between David's anointing as king to the day that he actually became king of Judah (he had to wait another seven years to become king over all Israel). Are we willing to wait fourteen years for God to accomplish what He has told us, or do we try and complete it ourselves? Sure, the first few years David may have thought that God would eventually fulfill His promise. Shortly after his anointing, David slew Goliath and that event propelled him to a leadership position in the army and a favorable position with the masses. This event was a high point in David's life and I am sure David could see God's hand guiding the situation towards its promised end. Waiting on God was probably easy for David during this time of progress. Shortly after this high point, King Saul turned on David and tried to chase him down and kill him. David was alone and fleeing for his life. Was David still sure that God would accomplish the task of making him king? Would we be sure?

The next couple of months David gathered a band of a few hundred men and was still running from Saul. He would be on the run for approximately eight years. The incredible part was—during that eight years David had two opportunities to kill Saul. In both instances Saul was totally helpless and all David had to do was finish Saul off. Even the people around David told David that God had given Saul into his hand and that David should take advantage of the circumstances. After all, God told David that he would be king so perhaps God orchestrated these circumstances to fulfill that end. The second incident went like this:

"So David and Abishai came to the people by night, and behold, Saul lay sleeping inside the circle of the camp with his spear stuck in the ground at his head; and Abner and the people were lying around him. Then Abishai said to David, 'Today God has delivered your enemy into your hand; now therefore, please let me strike him with the spear to the ground with one stroke, and I will not strike him the second time.' But David said to Abishai, 'Do not destroy him, for who can stretch out his hand against the LORD'S anointed and be without guilt?' David also said, 'As the LORD lives, surely the LORD will strike him, or his day will come that he dies, or he will go down into battle and perish. The LORD forbid that I should stretch out my hand against the LORD's anointed; but now please take the spear that is at his head and the jug of water, and let us go.'" (1 Samuel 26: 7-11)

David must have felt that God was forbidding him to proceed since on both occasions he did not slay Saul. David was waiting on God. Instead of getting the job done himself, David waited on God and watched for God's clear sign to proceed. David knew that he could get things done in his own power, but he dare not do what God wasn't leading him to do. Instead of lifting his own hand against God's anointed, David reasoned that God would deal with Saul when it was time. David, who had already been waiting for several years, chose to wait on God even longer. Would we be so patient?

During this time of waiting, God brought David through some high points and low points. In the process of waiting, God was training David while putting the pieces into place that would allow David to be a great king. Not only was David a great king, but God would establish an eternal kingdom through David. David would be the defining ancestor in the lineage of the Messiah.

For David, waiting was not a passive action or a time when nothing was accomplished. As he waited on God and grew in relationship with God, David penned some of his greatest psalms. Through this long process, God accomplished His goals for David's life AND grew a relationship with David at the same time. Although it may seem that nothing is happening when we wait on God, much is happening indeed! The very process of waiting on God is an exercise in faith and an exercise in sharpening our hearing. To this end, waiting on God is a way to give ourselves a "time out."

I have often heard people say, "Sometimes God doesn't give you instructions and you just have to proceed with what you know." While this is true, I think that in 99% of the cases the problem is not that God will not speak, but that we are not really waiting on Him long enough. In our drive through culture we expect that we can proceed right from the menu to the pick up window. We think that if we have waited on God for a week, then we have waited long enough! God is not on our schedule and waiting is not a passive action. He has given us instructions on how to live while waiting and we must carry these instructions out as a part of our training. If we are actively and obediently waiting on God, then there will be progress even while we are waiting. Waiting is not a state of doing nothing, waiting is a state of active obedience that is watching for God's signal to proceed. Waiting on God is not an excuse for indecision or laziness. After David became king, he was lounging around his castle when he should have been leading his troops in battle. Instead of watching for God's direction, he was watching Bathsheba in the tub. David, a man after God's own heart, fell into adultery and even murder. David was passively waiting, and in his laziness he looked to himself for direction instead of God. David hurt himself and those around him because he was not actively waiting on God.

Growing is a process in which we start off with baby steps. Perhaps you can relate to David's passive, sin-filled waiting and subsequent mess better than David's fourteen year wait to become king. Don't be discouraged, wherever you are is a good place to start. As a starting point, try to wait on God the next time you feel led to do something. For instance, you want to join a particular ministry at your church. Before you do anything, ask God to make it clear when you should proceed. Allow God to take the next weeks to sharpen your focus on HIM and not the task. When you should proceed, God will have people come up to you and ask you about it, He will strengthen your desires, and give you conviction and ideas. Most importantly, God will also have given you a better relationship with Him through this process. Waiting on God is stopping and tuning into the voice of God and His voice alone will prompt us to proceed. Waiting on God is also a way to discipline our fleshly appetite that hungers to get things done as quick as possible and in our own power. Waiting on God is the opposite of compulsive doing! Waiting on God is the necessary "time out" that brings us into closer relationship to God.

Questions to Ponder

What is your usual reaction to waiting? How can waiting change from an empty time into a time for growth?

How is waiting crucial to spiritual growth?

What is the difference between passive and active waiting? Can you think of examples of each from your life?

What are you waiting for? Has waiting changed your perspective towards it?

Part 5 Recap

As you build new habits, such as Sabbath keeping, journaling, being a monk, fighting the prayer snatchers, and waiting on God, remember that these practices are means to an end. The goal is to live in constant connection and attention to the voice of God. In order to overcome your compulsive doing and establish new habits of listening you must follow the biblical principle for overcoming sinful tendencies by focus and dependence on Christ. Perhaps some of the suggestions of this last section will help you build that focus.

Relax! If you have a relationship with Christ, you already have what you need. The key is to enjoy that relationship. Relaxing in Christ's assurance is like owning a pool in the summer. You have what you need to relax and cool off, all you have to do is jump in. You don't need to do more, just drop what you are doing and dive into the water. Take a "time out" and swim in the unfathomable depths of God and His love for you in Jesus. Maybe the suggestions in this section will get you into the water.

Do You Hear What I Hear?

Has God given you a "time out?" Can you see the guiding hand of God in your life as He tries to draw you closer to Him? We live in a culture that pushes us towards doing many things that distract us from God. We seek out the adrenaline rush and the esteem rush instead of seeking God. Sometimes even our churches push us towards doing tasks instead of knowing God. Despite all this misbehavior, we still have a loving Father in Heaven who is in control and who has not given up on us.

Perhaps as you read some of the precepts that God has shown me through my "time outs," you have seen the Father's loving hand in your life too. That is my hope. God has given me "time outs" because He is patient and steadfast in His love. God has given you "time outs" for the same reason. God has exposed my glaring weaknesses so that I will go to Him for strength. As I try my hardest and fail, as I listen to God and then ignore Him, as I raise children and try to be God's child—I see God's strong and steady hand pulling me back to His lap. It is true that sometimes I struggle to be let loose from His grip, but He holds me in "time out." Then, when I stop struggling, He whispers to me. The Father doesn't want to have to hold me from fleeing, but He will. What my Heavenly Father really desires is for me to go to Him at all times. He wants to love me, grow me, and make me into the man that He brought me into this world to be. God has said, "I will never leave you or forsake you." As I look over the course of my life I realize that this is the case indeed.

How about you? Can you see God's hand in the "time outs" of your life? Do you realize that God wants your ear and your heart? If you are His child through Christ, He will never leave you or forsake you. Will you stop bouncing around in the aisles of life with all those kids with chocolate-smeared faces? Will you stop acting so grown up and trying to fix all that you have broken? Will you run into the Father's arms and allow Him to raise you into who He made you to be? He made you to be His child, a child who has the qualities, the power, the love and the purpose of the Almighty Father in Heaven.

Questions to Ponder

What is the most important concept that you gleaned from this book?

How does your life need to change to implement that concept?

How do you plan to respond to your next "time out"?

Can you see God's hand in the "time outs" of your life?

End Notes

Assumptions

[1] Bernard of Clairvaux *Selected Works*, trans. by G.R. Evans (New York: Paulist Press, 1987) p. 187.

Giving You Your Do

[2] Sea monkeys are a registered trademark of Transcience Corp.
[3] Rick Warren, *The Purpose Driven Church* (Grand Rapids, MI.: Zondervan, 1995). *I am not criticizing Rick Warren. I think that the purpose driven model, like anything, can be used in a compulsive doing way or a redeemed relationship way. In his books, Warren tries to steer his readers into following the model in the right way.

Image is Everything

[4] Brennon Manning, *The Ragamuffin Gospel* (Sisters, OR: Multnomah Books, 2000).
[5] Brent Curtis and John Eldridge, *The Sacred Romance* (Nashville, TN: Thomas Nelson, 1997) p.85.
[6] Ibid.
[7] John Piper, *Desiring God* (Sisters, OR: Multnomah Books, 1996).
[8] A.W. Tozer, *The Knowledge of the Holy* (New York: Harper & Brothers, 1961).

The Biblical Principle for Breaking Bad Compulsions

[9] Donald Whitney, *Spiritual Disciplines For The Christian Life* (Colorado Springs: NavPress, 1991)   p. 19.

Becoming a Monk

[10] William of St. Thierry, *The Golden Epistle*, trans. by Theodore Berkeley (Kalamazoo, MI.: Cistercian Publications, 1980) pp. 18-19.

[11] Ibid. p.19.

[12] Brother Lawrence, *The Practice of the Presence of God* (Grand Rapids, MI: Spire Books, 2005)   pp. 29 – 30.

Invasion of the Prayer Snatchers

[13] William of St. Thierry, *The Golden Epistle*, trans. by Theodore Berkeley (Kalamazoo, MI.: Cistercian Publications, 1980) p. 34.

[14] Richard J. Foster, *Celebration of Discipline* (San Francisco: HarperSanFrancisco, 1988) p. 30.

Printed in the United States
49874LVS00002B/78

9 781424 103959